WILLIAMS
SONOMA

THE TIMELESS KITCHEN

100 Classic Recipes

DEVELOPED BY
WILLIAMS
SONOMA
TEST KITCHEN

weldonowen

Contents

The Bounty of the Garden

Vegetarian, Plant-Based, Salads, and Sides

The Flavors of the World

Global Flavors and Traditions

The Grill Master's Kitchen

Grilling Meat and Veggies

The Joy of Savory Baking
Loaves, Rolls, and Other Hearty Bakes

The Sweet Finale
Desserts for Every Occasion

The Art of Entertaining
Menus and Tips for Special Moments

Introduction
It all started with a dream.

In 1956, Chuck Williams opened the doors of Williams Sonoma with a simple vision: to bring the best cookware and culinary traditions of the world into American homes. From that dream grew a brand that has shaped how generations cook, gather, and celebrate.

This Platinum Anniversary Cookbook honors that legacy. Inside, you'll find 100 recipes that represent the very heart of Williams Sonoma, from beloved classics passed down by Chuck himself to fresh creations from our test-kitchen team. Together, they tell a story of heritage and innovation, of timeless flavors and new traditions waiting to be made.

As we celebrate our 70th anniversary, this book stands as both a tribute and an invitation: to cook with joy, to share generously, and to continue a tradition of bringing people together at the table.

Here's to the next chapter of cooking, celebrating, and making memories—together.

WILLIAMS
SONOMA

70 Years of Culinary Innovation
The Williams Sonoma Story

When Chuck Williams opened his first store in Sonoma, California, in 1956, he sparked a quiet revolution in American cooking. At a time when most kitchens were outfitted with only the basics, Chuck introduced home cooks to French copper pots, Italian espresso makers, and the kinds of tools used by professional chefs. His mission was simple yet transformative: If Americans had access to better tools, they would cook better–and enjoy it more.

From those early days, Williams Sonoma has been defined by innovation. Chuck's store wasn't just a place to shop; it was a place to discover. He introduced soufflé dishes when most Americans had never tasted one, popularized cookware from Europe long before it was mainstream, and encouraged adventurous cooking at home. In doing so, he reshaped the way a generation approached food.

Over the decades, this spirit of innovation has only grown. Williams Sonoma has embraced every wave of culinary evolution–from the rise of California cuisine and the farm-to-table movement to the surge of global flavors and modern techniques. Our test kitchen has been a proving ground for new ideas, translating professional-level tools and methods into recipes that inspire confidence and creativity in home cooks.

Yet, innovation at Williams Sonoma has never been about novelty for novelty's sake. It's about elevating everyday life. Whether through the introduction of the KitchenAid stand mixer to a new generation of bakers, the celebration of espresso culture at home, or today's exploration of sustainability and plant-forward cooking, we continue to champion products and recipes that make cooking more joyful, more meaningful, and more connected to the way people live now.

Seventy years later, Chuck's vision endures: Cooking is not just a skill but an experience–a way to gather, to celebrate, and to care for one another. Williams Sonoma remains at the forefront of culinary culture because we never stop asking what will inspire cooks next. From heritage recipes to cutting-edge techniques, from timeless tools to modern innovations, we've spent seven decades shaping how America cooks–and we're just getting started.

The Essential Kitchen Tools and Pantry

A well-stocked kitchen is the foundation of great cooking. In this chapter, you'll find the must-have tools and pantry staples that make everyday cooking easier, more efficient, and more enjoyable. From durable cookware and sharp knives to oils, spices, and grains, these essentials set you up for success, whether you're preparing a quick weeknight meal or hosting a special occasion.

Bakeware Materials

Pans are available in several different materials, each with their own advantages and disadvantages.

Aluminum—An even heat conductor that browns baked goods uniformly and cools quickly. Anodized aluminum is more durable and resists corrosion; insulated aluminum heats more slowly, reducing the risk of burnt bottoms.

Cast Iron—Durable cast iron absorbs and releases heat more slowly than other metals, turning out delicate muffins with fine, thin crusts and moist interiors.

Glass and Ceramic—These materials, used mainly for baking dishes and pie dishes or plates, encourage browning because the radiant heat is conducted and retained well by them. Foods bake more quickly in glass and ceramic bakeware, too, so you may need to reduce baking times and temperatures.

Nonstick—A nonstick coating ensures the easy release of baked goods and quick cleanup. Nonstick aluminum is a good heat conductor but is not always as sturdy as other materials, such as nonstick heavy-gauge steel. Look for a double-layer nonstick coating and remember to use wooden or plastic utensils to avoid scratching the surface.

Stainless Steel—Heavy-gauge stainless steel is strong and easy to clean, a good choice for bakeware. Tinned steel is used in classic French baking; the shiny surface provided by the tin prevents overbrowning. Darkened steel pans, the choice of many professional bakers, are excellent absorbers and distributors of heat.

Baking Vessels

Baking Dish—Used for everything from brownies to small roasts and lasagna, deep glass dishes (or metal pans) come in all shapes and sizes, but for the average home baker the most common are a 9-by-13-by-2-inch (23 by 33 by 5 cm) rectangular dish and an 8- or 9-inch (20 or 23 cm) square dish with 2-inch (5 cm) sides.

Baking Sheet—This rectangular metal pan with shallow, slightly sloping rims comes in several forms. The jellyroll pan, so named because it is used to make sponge cakes that, after baking, are spread with a filling such as jelly and then rolled, is 10 by 15 inches (25 by 37.5 cm) with ½-inch (13 mm) rims. Half-sheet pans are 12 by 17 inches (30 by 42.5 cm), half the size of large commercial baking sheets. Baking sheets are handy for making rolls or croissants or may be used as roasting pans for small cuts of meat.

Cake Pan—Plan to buy at least two round cake pans in the sizes you are likely to use: 1½ to 2 inches (4 to 5 cm) deep and 8 or 9 inches (20 or 23 cm) in diameter. American cake pans are not as deep as European ones. Choose good-quality, seamless, heavy metal pans. Square and rectangular pans are also called for in some recipes.

Cookie Sheet—A flat metal pan, usually with a low rim on one or two ends, designed to allow for sliding cookies onto a cooking rack. Avoid very dark sheets, which will cause your baked goods to burn. Nonstick cookie sheets work well and are very easy to clean. Insulated cookie sheets, which have an interior air pocket between two layers of metal, guarantee that no cookie will ever have an overbrowned bottom. They do not, however, work well for thin, crisp cookies, which benefit from intense heat.

Loaf Pan—Also called a bread pan, a standard loaf pan is 5 by 9 by 3 inches (12.5 by 23 by 7.5 cm) and may be metal or glass. A small pan, 4½ by 8½ by 2½ inches (11.5 by 21.5 by 6.5 cm), is also useful. Metal loaf pans produce loaf cakes and quick breads with evenly browned crusts; glass dishes encourage fast browning, sometimes at the expense of the interior of the bread or cake. Can also be used for meatloaf.

Muffin Pan—Standard muffin and cupcake pans typically have six or twelve cups, each holding 6 to 7 tablespoons (90 to 105 g) of batter. Jumbo and miniature "gem" pans are also available. Cups can be lined with paper or greased, though paper may cause the crust to stick. Specialty pans include wide, flat cups for thin, crisp muffins and whimsical or holiday shapes like hearts, stars, or dinosaurs. Aluminum and steel are common, but nonstick cast-iron pans are ideal.

Pie Pan—Buy metal pie pans or glass or ceramic pie plates in 9- and 10-inch (23 and 25 cm) sizes. Glass pie plates let you see how the bottom crust is browning, although they are sometimes overzealous heat conductors that lead to a brown crust and an undercooked middle. Look for a wide rim to hold up the fluted edge of the crust.

Baking Tools

From sturdy mixing bowls and precise measuring cups to reliable spatulas and a well-loved stand mixer, the right baking tools turn simple ingredients into something extraordinary.

Cookie and Biscuit Cutters—Although some are made from plastic, the best cutters are made of metal, so that the cutting side holds its edge. Cookie cutters come in different shapes and sizes, from the basic round to holiday icons and seasonal themes. Biscuit cutters are round and often fluted and may come in nests of graduated sizes.

Cooling Rack—Because cakes, cookies, pies, and breads should be allowed to cool evenly with air circulating on all sides, recipes call for cooling baked goods on wire racks. Most are made of chrome-plated metal, although some are made from stainless steel or nonstick aluminum. Have on hand two or three racks. You'll want enough to handle two cake layers or two sheets of cookies.

Dough Scraper—Also called a bench scraper, this tool lifts and divides dough, scrapes boards, and transfers chopped ingredients. Most have wooden or plastic handles with stainless-steel or plastic blades, usually rectangular with sometimes rounded corners. Choose a sturdy, hefty metal scraper for durability.

Frosting Spatula—Also called an icing spatula or a pastry spatula, this long, flat metal utensil with its slender, flexible blade 6 to 12 inches (15 to 30.5 cm) long resembles a round-tipped knife without a sharp edge. When the handle angles off the blade, the spatula is called an offset spatula. Both types will make frosting your cakes easier.

Mixing Bowls–Stocking bowls in a range of materials, shapes, and sizes will help you tackle varied tasks more efficiently. For example, whipping egg whites and creaming butter call for deep bowls, while preparing and organizing ingredients for a cake call for a range of smaller bowls.

Mixing Spoons–Wooden mixing spoons, favored for their sturdiness and heat resistance, should be made of hardwoods like beech or ash. Keep separate spoons for baking and savory use and have various sizes for different tasks. Stainless-steel and sturdy plastic options are also available.

Pastry Blender–Also known as a dough blender, this tool transforms fat and flour into a consistency suitable for pastry dough. It has a wooden or plastic handle anchoring a row of steel wires forming a U shape. The wires act as cutters, reducing pieces of butter or other fat to the size of small peas or the consistency of meal.

Pastry Brush–This important tool is used to brush water, egg washes, melted butter, or glazes on pastry. The brushes are made with natural or nylon bristles, with the latter usually no more than 1½ inches (4 cm) long and 1 to 2 inches (2.5 to 5 cm) wide. Goose-feather brushes are excellent for egg washes. Wash pastry brushes in hot, soapy water and keep them separate from brushes used for savory foods.

Rolling Pin–Rolling pins come in various sizes and materials, with choice largely a matter of preference. Heavy, smooth wooden pins are ideal for most doughs; French-style pins lack handles, while others have them. Professional pins often feature ball bearings for smooth rolling. Marble or stainless-steel pins stay cool, and some even have hollow centers for ice, though that may be unnecessary.

Rubber Spatula–Also called a bowl scraper, this tool is ideal for scraping bowls, spreading batters, or scooping the contents out of containers. Silicone blades are best, as they resist heat and sticking; smaller sizes are also available.

Sifter–A canister with mesh screens and a rotating blade for sifting and aerating flour, cocoa, or sugar. Available in 1- to 8-cup (240 g to 1.9 kg) sizes, with 2 to 3 cups (480 to 720 g) most practical.

Whisk–Wire whisks range from 6 to 12 inches (15 to 30.5 cm) and come in three main types: sauce whisks with stiff wires for thorough mixing, balloon whisks with rounded heads for incorporating air, and flat whisks for gravies and sauces. The best are made with stainless-steel wires and sealed handles to prevent food from collecting.

Cookware Materials

The most important long-term investment the home cook makes is in cookware. As with all kitchen equipment, look for solid construction that will last a lifetime.

Aluminum–Heats rapidly and evenly, is durable and relatively inexpensive, but reacts with acidic foods and can impart a metallic taste. It also tends to warp if not of sufficient gauge. Select anodized aluminum, which has been treated with an electrolytic process to make it harder, denser, and resistant to corrosion.

Cast Iron–Heats more slowly than some other materials but holds the heat extremely well and uniformly, even at high temperatures, making it

LA COCOTTE
STAUB
STAUB
STAUB

good for frying and searing. It reacts with acidic foods and can impart a metallic taste. Regular cast iron is heavy and should always be dried after washing to prevent rusting. Enameled cast iron holds heat extremely well and is good for long, slow cooking but is prone to chipping and staining.

Copper–Heats and cools rapidly and evenly. Many cooks feel copper is the preferred metal for cookware. Copper cookware must be lined to avoid reactions with foods. Copper pans with stainless steel interiors and alloyed-aluminum and aluminum cores, which are durable and handsome, are a good compromise.

Nonstick–These popular coatings have steadily improved over the years. Unlike in the past, coatings today do not affect the metal's ability to conduct heat. In addition, they are durable and very easy to clean. Keep in mind that although nonstick is helpful for making omelets, oatmeal, and rice, it will interfere with browning meat.

Stainless Steel–Does not react with acidic ingredients and will not corrode, but it is a poor absorber of heat. Cladded stainless steel–that is, stainless steel exterior with a carbon core–boasts rapid and uniform heat conduction. Stainless steel with a layered alloyed-aluminum and aluminum core or an aluminum disk bottom also heats quickly and evenly, does not corrode, and is durable.

Cooking Vessels

Double Boiler–A set of two pans, one nesting atop the other, outfitted with one lid that fits both pans. A small amount of water is barely simmered in the lower pan, while ingredients are placed in the top pan to heat them gently, keep them warm, or melt them.

Dutch Oven–Large round or oval pots with tight-fitting lids and two loop handles used for slow cooking on top of the stove or in the oven. Most are made of enameled cast iron, although some are made of regular cast iron or other uncoated metals. They range from 4 to 12 quarts (3.9 to 10.8 L); 8 or 9 quarts (7.2 or 8.1 L) is recommended for most home kitchens.

Griddle–Flat rectangles or rounds of cast iron or cast aluminum, often with a nonstick finish, griddles sit flat on the stove top and are designed to be heated over one or two burners. They are used to cook pancakes, eggs, bacon, thick steaks, cheese sandwiches, and more. Most have depressed rims to catch grease.

Saucepan–Saucepans are round pans with straight or sloping sides, typically 1 to 5 quarts (1 to 4.5 L); 2 quarts (1.8 L) is most versatile. Traditional saucepans are twice as wide as tall for quick evaporation. Straight-sided saucepans suit long cooking, while slant-sided "chef's pans" speed sauce reduction. Anodized aluminum or aluminized steel are best.

Sauté Pan–Sauté pans, or straight-sided frying pans, have high sides (2½ to 4 inches [6.5 to 10 cm]) and an angled handle to keep food contained while flipping. Ideal for braising or liquid-rich dishes, they range 6 to 14½ inches (15 to 37 cm) in diameter and 1 to 7 quarts (1 to 6.3 L) in capacity, with 2½ to 4 quarts (2.3 to 3.6 L) most practical. Many come with lids.

Skillet–A skillet, or frying pan, has outward-flaring sides for stirring or turning food. Kitchens typically have a small (9 to 10 inches [23 to 25 cm]) and large (12 to 14 inches [30.5 to 35.5 cm]) skillet.

Skillets lack lids; anodized aluminum or cast iron are best, with one ideally nonstick.

Stockpot—Also knowns as a spaghetti pot or soup pot, a stockpot is a high, narrow pot designed for minimal evaporation during cooking. Stockpots are fitted with tight-fitting lids and two looped handles for easy lifting. They should be made of heavy-gauge metal with good heft. The smallest stockpots have an 8-quart (7.2 L) capacity. Most home cooks find stockpots with 10- to 12-quart (9 to 10.8 L) capacities to be the most useful.

Wok—This ingenious Chinese pan is a versatile cooking device ideal for stir-frying, deep-frying, and steaming. Traditionally made of plain steel, a good retainer of heat, the wok has a rounded bottom that allows small pieces of food to be rapidly tossed and stirred, while the gradually sloping sides help keep the food inside the pan.

Cooking Tools

Boning Knife—About the length of a utility knife, this tool has a very narrow, curve-edged blade that maneuvers more easily around the bones of raw poultry or meat.

Bread Knife—A straight, serrated blade at least 8 inches (20 cm) long. The serrated edge cuts easily through the tough crusts of breads or through the delicate skins of tomatoes that might otherwise be crushed by an ordinary knife.

Chef's Knife—A larger, evenly proportioned, tapered blade, of which the most useful usually average 8 inches (20 cm) long. Most often used for chopping as well as for slicing, dicing, julienning, or mincing ingredients.

Garlic Press—A garlic press minces peeled cloves for easy mixing. It has a hinged perforated hopper and plunger, with some featuring a tool to push out waste or a storage tube. Simple metal models are the most effective.

Knife—Knife sharpness ensures efficient, safe cutting. Modern carbon-stainless steel blades sharpen well, resist rust, and outperform traditional carbon steel. Handles—wood, resin-impregnated wood, plastic, or rubber—should be securely riveted and the knife well balanced.

Mandoline—A mandoline is a flat, rectangular slicer with smooth or corrugated blades for slicing, julienning, or waffle-cutting. It ensures precise, uniform cuts. Designs vary—some rest on a bowl, others have foldaway legs for ergonomic use. Choose one with a hand guard for safety.

Meat Mallet—A mallet is useful for pounding boneless meat and poultry pieces until thin for quick and even cooking. Also called a meat pounder, although pounders tend to have one smooth side for flattening only, while mallets often have two sides, one with blunt teeth that help break down fibers in the meat, thus tenderizing it.

Mortar and Pestle—This primitive pair of tools used for pounding and grinding ingredients consists of a sturdy bowl-shaped mortar and a heavy, cylindrical pounder or pestle. While their work is often replaced nowadays by mechanized tools such as spice mills and food processors, the duo remains an excellent way to grind up spices or nuts, or to pound garlic together with fresh basil and pine nuts for pesto sauce at its most rustic. The best material for a mortar is marble, which is heavy, sturdy, and will not absorb food odors; heavy-duty ceramic models are also good.

Paring Knife—A small, evenly proportioned, tapered blade usually 3 to 4 inches (7.5 to 10 cm) long. Used for paring and slicing fruits and vegetables and for chopping small quantities.

Potato Ricer—A useful device for making smooth mashed potatoes and similar dishes. A plunger pushes potatoes through a perforated basket, reducing them to the consistency of grains of rice that are then stirred into a fluffy mass.

Slicing Knife—A long, slender, fairly flexible blade, well adapted to carving roast poultry and whole fish.

Steamer Basket—Also called vegetable or folding steamers, these collapsible perforated metal baskets adjust to fit various pans and sit on small feet to hold food above simmering water, allowing steam to circulate evenly.

Tongs—Tongs, typically 10 to 12 inches (25 to 30.5 cm) long, have blunt ends for grasping food and may feature finger loops or V-shaped tips for control. Longer versions are useful for grilling and often include a lock for storage. They're ideal for handling hot food, turning meat, tossing salads, checking pasta, and plating.

Utility Knife—Similar to a paring knife but slightly larger, with a blade 6 to 8 inches (15 to 20 cm) long. Used for peeling and slicing or for carving small cuts of meat.

Zester—The citrus zester's metal blade at the end of a short handle is fitted with a row of four to six sharp-edged holes that allow for the removal of thin strips of the colorful outermost part of the peel while leaving behind the bitter white pith.

Small Appliances

Food Processor—Food processors are versatile, powerful kitchen tools. They feature a straight-sided bowl on a motorized base, with a central rotating shaft for an S-shaped blade that chops, blends, mixes, and purées. Attachments include disks for slicing, shredding, grating, julienning, and a blade for kneading dough, with a feed tube for adding ingredients while the machine is running.

Immersion Blenders—Immersion blenders, or handheld blenders, use an extended blade that blends food directly in its cooking or mixing container, allowing for larger batches than a standing blender. They incorporate more air, useful for frothy soups, usually have two speeds, and must be fully immersed to avoid spattering.

Multicooker—This versatile electric appliance combines pressure cooking, slow cooking, rice making, sautéing, and steaming in one unit. Perfect for quick weeknight dinners or hands-off weekend cooking, it dramatically reduces cooking times for braises and stews while allowing you to brown ingredients directly in the pot for maximum flavor development.

Pressure Cooker—This special cooking pot is equipped with an airtight locking lid that forces pressure to build up inside the pot as the liquid within it comes to a boil. The trapped steam causes the internal temperature to rise beyond what it would be capable of doing in a covered pot, decreasing cooking times by two-thirds or more.

Standing Blenders—Blenders feature a sturdy base housing an electric motor and a lidded jar (5 to 8 cups [1.2 to 1.9 kg]) with a blade at the bottom. Most lids include a removable 2-ounce (60 g) cap for adding liquid while blending. Depending on the model, blenders may have two to sixteen or more speeds.

Pantry Essentials

Building and maintaining a solid pantry foundation transforms how you cook. Stock it with essentials—dried pasta, rice, flour, canned goods, oils, vinegars, and core spices—and you'll always be able to create satisfying meals, even when the refrigerator looks bare. Beyond convenience, a well-curated pantry reduces waste, saves money, and gives you freedom to cook intuitively, experimenting without being tied to recipes or shopping lists.

Oils and Fats

Extra Virgin Olive Oil (for finishing)

Olive Oil (for cooking)

Toasted Sesame Oil

Neutral Oil (Avocado, Sunflower, or Canola)

Oil Spray (for baking)

Ghee

Duck Fat or Lard

Vinegars

Balsamic Vinegar

Red Wine Vinegar

White Wine Vinegar

Apple Cider Vinegar

Sherry Vinegar

Rice Wine Vinegar

Salt and Peppers

Coarse Kosher Salt

Flake Salt

Black Peppercorns

Infused Salts

MSG

Spices and Herbs

Garlic Powder or Granulated Garlic

Onion Powder or Granulated Onion

Dried Oregano

Dried Basil

Dried Thyme

Dried Rosemary

Dried Bay Leaves

Crushed Red Pepper Flakes

Smoked Paprika

Sweet Paprika

Chili Powder

Ground Ginger

Ground Allspice

Ground Cumin

Ground Coriander

Ground or Whole Cardamom

Cayenne

Cinnamon Sticks

Chinese 5-Spice

Ground Cinnamon

Fennel Seeds

Mustard Seeds

Whole Nutmeg

Canned and Jarred

Anchovy Paste or Anchovies

Canned Tuna (in olive oil)

Capers

Canned Sun-Dried Tomatoes

Canned Artichoke Hearts

Canned or Packaged Beans (Cannellini, Chickpeas, Black Beans)

Vegetable, Chicken and Beef Broth (cubes or liquid)

Canned Tomatoes (whole peeled)

Canned Coconut Milk

Tomato Paste

Olives

Pickles / Cornichons

Tahini

Sauces and Sweeteners

Worcestershire Sauce

Dijon Mustard

Mayonnaise

Hot Sauce

Honey

Maple Syrup

Tomato Sauce

Ketchup

Dried

Pasta

Couscous

Arborio Rice

Jasmine Rice

Polenta

Dried Mushrooms

Breadcrumbs/Panko

Lentils

Global

Sambal

Oyster Sauce

Gochujang

Gochugaru

Sichuan Peppercorns

Dried Chiles

Tamari or Soy Sauce (or Coconut Aminos)

Fish Sauce

Ponzu Sauce

Dashi

Curry Paste

Miso Paste

Calabrian Chile Paste

Black Rice Vinegar

Tamarind Paste

Coconut or Palm Sugar

Mirin

Baking

Baking Powder

Baking Soda

All Purpose Flour

Almond Flour

Cornstarch

Brown Sugar

White Sugar

Vanilla Extract/Paste

Yeast

Powdered Sugar

Cocoa Powder

Cream of Tartar

Semi-Sweet Chocolate

d'arbo
since 1879
DERFLOWER
SYRUP
Dilute 1+8
refreshing drink,
part (40 mL) of this
drink mix with 8 parts
Indulge yourself!
syrup can also
on pancakes or ice
for a delicious treat.
before use.
after opening.
FL OZ (1 PT 0.9 FL OZ)
500 ML

The Home Bar

Hosting Memorable Gatherings

Creating exceptional drinks at home isn't about fancy tools or rare spirits—it's about balance, fresh ingredients, and the joy of sharing something special. A Classic Margarita brings bright simplicity, a Maple Bourbon Smash adds warmth and depth, and a Limoncello Spritz keeps things light and celebratory. Whether it's a dinner for two or a lively gathering, the right cocktail sets the tone for laughter, conversation, and genuine connection.

Blood Orange Negroni (aka Sicilian Negroni)

Blood oranges, such as the Tarocco and Moro varieties from Sicily, Italy, are prized for their ruby-red flesh, which adds a dramatic color to local desserts, salads, and drinks. The juice is a perfect addition to a classic Negroni, as it beautifully complements the orange flavor of the Campari.

MAKES 1 SERVING

1½ ounces (45 ml) fresh blood orange juice or orange juice

1 ounce (30 ml) gin

1 ounce (30 ml) Campari

¾ ounce (23 ml) sweet vermouth

Dash of orange bitters

1 ounce (30 ml) Prosecco or sparkling water

Orange twist, for garnish

In a mixing glass or cocktail shaker filled with ice, combine the orange juice, gin, Campari, vermouth, and bitters. Stir or shake until well chilled, about 30 seconds, then strain into a tumbler filled with fresh ice. Top with the Prosecco, garnish with the orange twist, and serve.

Maple Bourbon Smash

This elegantly simple cocktail balances the warmth of bourbon with the natural sweetness of maple syrup and the brightness of fresh lemon juice. It's perfectly refreshing yet sophisticated—ideal for fall evenings or anytime you want a drink that feels both seasonal and timeless.

MAKES 1 SERVING

- 2 ounces (60 ml) bourbon
- 1 ounce (30 ml) maple syrup
- 1 ounce (30 ml) fresh lemon juice
- Lemon twist, for garnish

Pour the bourbon, maple syrup, and lemon juice into a shaker filled with ice. Shake until the drink is thoroughly chilled, about 20 seconds. Strain into a double old-fashioned glass with a large cube of ice. Garnish with the lemon twist and serve immediately.

If desired, smoke the cocktail with applewood chips for 15 seconds using a handheld cocktail smoker (such as a Crafthouse Smoking Box), or until the desired amount of smokiness is achieved.

French 75

This Champagne cocktail was named for a French field gun, as the original mix was said to carry an artillery-like kick. Here, the power of the French 75 is tempered with a double dose of fragrant lavender.

MAKES 1 SERVING

1 ounce (30 ml) gin

½ ounce (15 ml) lavender simple syrup

½ ounce (15 ml) fresh lemon juice

2 ounces (60 ml) Champagne or sparkling wine

2 fresh lavender sprigs

Lemon twist, for garnish

In a cocktail shaker filled with ice, combine the gin, lavender simple syrup, and lemon juice. Cover, shake vigorously, and strain into a Champagne flute. Top with the Champagne. Garnish with the lavender sprigs and lemon twist and serve.

Lavender Simple Syrup

2 cups (16 fl. oz./500 ml) water

3 tablespoons dried lavender

2 cups (1 lb./500 g) sugar

In a saucepan over medium-high heat, combine the water and lavender and bring to a boil. Add the sugar and cook, stirring, until the sugar is completely dissolved. Remove from the heat and let the lavender steep in the liquid for 30 minutes to 1 hour. Pour the liquid through a fine-mesh sieve into a clear jar, pressing on the lavender with the back of a spoon to extract any liquid. Use immediately or cover and store in the refrigerator for up to 1 week.

Spanish G&T

Be generous when garnishing this cocktail classic. Take inspiration from Spanish bartenders, who traditionally pile on flowers, herbs, and spices to amplify the botanical flavors in the gin.

MAKES 1 SERVING

- 4 ounces (120 ml) tonic water
- 2 ounces (60 ml) gin
- 2 dashes Angostura bitters
- Grapefruit slice, juniper berries, lemon twist, edible flowers, and/or fresh rosemary sprig, for garnish

Fill a rocks glass with ice. Add the tonic water, gin, and Angostura bitters and stir to combine. Garnish with a slice of grapefruit and your choice of juniper berries, a lemon twist, edible flowers, or a fresh rosemary sprig. Serve.

Classic Moijito

Crafted with light rum, lime juice, fresh muddled mint, and sparkling water, the mojito is a timeless cocktail that's especially cooling on warm days. If sugar cubes aren't available, you can substitute a spoonful of superfine sugar or a splash of Simple Syrup (page 33).

MAKES 1 SERVING

2 sugar cubes
Sparkling water, as needed
6 fresh mint leaves
1½ ounces (45 ml) light rum
Juice of 1 small lime
Mint sprig, for garnish
Lime wheel, for garnish

In a mixing glass, combine the sugar cubes, a splash of sparkling water, and the mint leaves. Using a muddler, lightly crush the contents of the glass until the mint is aromatic and the sugar is dissolved. Add the rum and lime juice to the glass, fill the glass with ice, and stir until well chilled. Strain the contents of the glass into a double old fashioned or highball glass filled with fresh ice and top off with more sparkling water. Garnish with the mint sprig and lime wheel and serve immediately.

Classic Margarita

There are almost as many recipes for margaritas as there are aficionados of tequila. You'll find them served up blended with ice or made with a variety of fruits such as watermelon or mango. Here is a classic version of the drink, served on ice to keep it cold on warm summer evenings.

MAKES 2 SERVINGS

Coarse sea salt for the glasses

1 lime wedge

3 ounces (90 ml) white tequila

1 ounce (30 ml) Cointreau or triple sec

1 ounce (30 ml) fresh lime juice

2 lime wheels for garnish (optional)

Spread the salt on a small plate. Moisten the rims of two small tumblers or two margarita glasses with the lime wedge. One at a time, invert the glasses onto the plate to coat the rims, then shake off any excess salt. Fill the glasses with ice.

In a cocktail shaker filled with ice, combine the tequila, Cointreau, and lime juice. Shake vigorously for 15 seconds. Strain into the prepared glasses and garnish each glass with a lime wheel. Serve immediately.

Moscow Mule

Traditionally served in a copper mug to keep it ice-cold, the Moscow Mule can also be served in a highball glass. For a perfectly chilled drink, freeze your mug for a few hours beforehand.

MAKES 1 SERVING

1½ ounces (45 ml) vodka

½ ounce (15 ml) fresh lime juice

¼ ounce (7 ml) Simple Syrup (this page)

3 to 4 ounces (90 to 120 ml) ginger beer

Fresh mint sprig, for garnish

In a cocktail shaker filled with ice, combine the vodka, lime juice, and simple syrup. Cover, shake vigorously, and strain into an ice-filled copper mug or highball glass. Top with the ginger beer to taste and stir gently. Garnish with the mint sprig and serve immediately.

Simple Syrup

MAKES 2 CUPS (480 ML)

1 cup (240 ml) water

1 cup (200 g) sugar

In a small saucepan over medium-high heat, bring the water to a simmer. Add the sugar and stir until it completely dissolves. Remove the pan from the heat and set aside to cool to room temperature. Pour the syrup into a clean 1-pint (480 ml) bottle, cap it, and refrigerate until ready to use. Can be stored for about 3 to 4 weeks refrigerated in a clean, airtight container.

Pomegranate Cosmopolitan

This cocktail is a vibrant and flavorful twist on the classic cosmopolitan. The addition of pomegranate juice gives it a richer, more complex sweetness and a deeper color, making it a sophisticated choice for any occasion.

MAKES 1 SERVING

1½ ounces (45 ml) good-quality vodka, such as Grey Goose or Finlandia

¾ ounce (23 ml) orange liqueur, such as Cointreau

¾ ounce (23 ml) cranberry juice cocktail, such as Ocean Spray

½ ounce (15 ml) bottled pomegranate juice, such as Pom Wonderful

½ ounce (15 ml) fresh lime juice (from about ⅓ lime)

Lime wheel or twist, for garnish

Fill a cocktail shaker with ice. Add the vodka, orange liqueur, cranberry juice, pomegranate juice, and lime juice. Shake vigorously until the outside of the shaker is thoroughly chilled. Strain the mixture into a chilled martini or coupe glass. Garnish with a fresh lime wheel or twist and serve.

Lychee Lemonade

With its gentle floral sweetness and hint of tropical fragrance, lychee syrup brings excitement to this alcohol-free drink that's ideal for spring gatherings. You can find the syrup online, at liquor stores, and at specialty food markets.

MAKES 1 SERVING

2 ounces (60 ml) lychee syrup

¾ ounce (23 ml) fresh lemon juice

½ ounce (15 g) sugar

Pinch of kosher salt

2 ounces (60 ml) water

Fresh mint leaf, for garnish

Lemon wheel, for garnish

Chill a cocktail glass in the freezer for at least 20 minutes.

In a blender, combine the lychee syrup, lemon juice, sugar, salt, water, and a handful of ice. Blend on high speed until thoroughly combined, 10 to 15 seconds.

Fill the chilled glass with crushed ice. Strain the lychee mixture into the glass, garnish with a mint leaf and lemon wheel, and serve immediately.

Coconut Cream Margarita

Blanco tequila, a clear and unaged spirit, gets a rich and creamy texture here from coconut cream. This combines with the standard margarita ingredients—orange liqueur and lime juice—for a unique twist.

MAKES 1 SERVING

- Kosher salt, grated lime zest, and sugar, for rimming glass
- 2 lime wedges
- 2 ounces (60 ml) coconut cream or cream of coconut
- 1½ ounces (45 ml) blanco tequila
- 1 ounce (30 ml) fresh lime juice
- ½ ounce (15 ml) Cointreau
- ¼ ounce (7 ml) Simple Syrup (page 33)

On a small plate, combine equal parts salt, lime zest, and sugar and spread in an even layer. Gently rub 1 of the lime wedges around the rim of a rocks glass. Holding the base of the glass, dip the rim into the salt mixture. Place in the refrigerator until ready to use.

Just before serving, fill the glass with ice. In a cocktail shaker filled with ice, combine the coconut cream, tequila, lime juice, Cointreau, and simple syrup. Cover, shake vigorously until well chilled, and strain into the ice-filled glass. Garnish with the remaining lime wedge and serve.

Limoncello Spritz

Sparkling wine means it's time to celebrate, and this bright, refreshing cocktail offers a perfect way to toast the new season. Drawing inspiration from the classic Italian Aperol spritz—which showcases the vibrant orange, bittersweet liqueur Aperol—we've substituted limoncello to deliver concentrated citrus flavor ideal for spring. Aromatic ginger beer contributes a spicy finishing note.

MAKES 1 SERVING

2 ounces (60 ml) limoncello

½ ounce (15 ml) ginger beer

¼ ounce (7 ml) fresh lemon juice

½ ounce (15 ml) soda water

3 ounces (90 ml) Prosecco or other sparkling wine

Fresh mint sprig, for garnish

Lemon slice, for garnish

Fill a wineglass half full with ice. Add the limoncello, ginger beer, and lemon juice. Top with the soda water and Prosecco and stir to combine. Garnish with a mint sprig and lemon slice and serve immediately.

Hibiscus Elderflower Basil Spritz

While a spritz usually features sparkling wine, it's simple to create a nonalcoholic version like this one. We blend hibiscus tea with floral elderflower syrup, fresh basil, and a hint of honey, then add effervescence with SodaStream carbonated water. Served over ice, this refreshing crimson beverage is ideal for summer sipping.

MAKES 2 SERVINGS

16 ounces (480 ml) water

4 hibiscus tea bags or ¼ ounce (7 g) loose-leaf tea

¼ ounce (7 ml) local wildflower honey, or more as needed

8 large fresh basil leaves

1 ounce (30 ml) store-bought elderflower syrup, preferably made with honey

2 pineapple slices, for garnish

Place 2 tall tumbler glasses in the freezer to chill for about 1 hour before serving.

Meanwhile, in a small saucepan over high heat, bring 12 ounces (360 ml) of the water to a simmer. Remove from the heat and add the hibiscus tea. Let the tea steep for 10 minutes or according to the package instructions. Remove the tea bags and pour the tea into a pitcher; if using loose-leaf tea, strain the tea into the pitcher. While the tea is still warm, whisk in the honey until dissolved. Let the tea cool at room temperature. Taste and adjust the sweetness with more honey if desired. The tea can be stored in an airtight container in the refrigerator for up to 4 days.

Pour the remaining 4 ounces (120 ml) of water into a SodaStream bottle. Insert the bottle into the SodaStream machine and set to maximum fizz according to the manufacturer's instructions. Once the water has carbonated, remove the bottle from the machine, pour the carbonated water into the pitcher with the tea, and stir gently to combine.

To serve, add 4 basil leaves to the bottom of each chilled tumbler. Pour ½ ounce (15 ml) of the elderflower syrup over the basil leaves in each tumbler. Lightly muddle the basil and syrup until the flavors are combined but the basil leaves aren't fully crushed. Add a handful of ice cubes over the muddled basil, then pour the hibiscus tea over the ice, filling the glasses to the top. Garnish each tumbler with a pineapple slice, add a straw, if desired, and serve immediately.

The Art of the Appetizer

Hors d'Oeuvres, Small Plates, and Dips

Great appetizers serve a dual purpose: They're the gracious host's secret weapon for buying time while final preparations are made, and they're the perfect icebreaker that gets guests mingling and talking. Whether you're planning an intimate cocktail hour or a grand celebration, these recipes offer something for every occasion and skill level. The delicate Phyllo Cups with Caviar and Crème Fraîche (page 51) speak to special occasions, while our beloved Deviled Eggs Three Ways (page 56) proves that even the most familiar favorites can be elevated into something extraordinary.

Mini Crab Cakes with Lemon Aioli

Perfect crab cakes deliver a crispy exterior, tender interior, and bold, fresh seafood taste. While many recipes rely too heavily on fillers, these generous cakes showcase sweet crabmeat as the star, using just enough additional ingredients to enhance flavor and provide structure without overwhelming the delicate crustacean.

MAKES 8 CRAB CAKES, 4 SERVINGS

LEMON AIOLI

1 cup (240 g) mayonnaise

Finely grated zest of 1 lemon

2 tablespoons (30 ml) fresh lemon juice

1 garlic clove, minced

Fine sea salt and freshly ground pepper

CRAB CAKES

1 pound (450 g) fresh-cooked lump crabmeat

¾ cup (90 g) panko or other dried breadcrumbs

1 egg, beaten

1 tablespoon (15 ml) Dijon mustard

2 teaspoons Worcestershire sauce

¼ teaspoon hot pepper sauce

1 tablespoon (3 g) chopped fresh flat-leaf parsley

½ cup (120 ml) canola oil

Lemon wedges, for serving

To make the aioli: Combine the mayonnaise, lemon zest, lemon juice, and garlic in a small bowl. Season with salt and pepper, then reserve ¼ cup (60 g) and refrigerate the remainder until serving.

To make the crab cakes: Line a rimmed baking sheet with parchment paper. Carefully check the crabmeat for any shell fragments or cartilage. In a bowl, combine ¼ cup (30 g) of the panko with the reserved aioli, egg, mustard, Worcestershire sauce, hot pepper sauce, and parsley. Gently fold in the crabmeat until just combined. Form the mixture into 8 equal portions, shaping each into a thick cake. Place the remaining ½ cup (60 g) of panko in a shallow dish, coat each cake evenly, and arrange on the prepared baking sheet. Chill for 15 minutes.

Heat the oil in a large frying pan over medium-high heat until shimmering. Cook the cakes until golden brown on the bottom, 2 to 3 minutes, then flip and cook until the second side is golden, about 2 minutes more. Transfer to paper towels using a slotted spatula and drain briefly. Serve immediately with lemon wedges and the remaining aioli alongside.

VARIATIONS

Replace the aioli with homemade mayonnaise or a simple lemon vinaigrette. For green goddess dressing, whisk together 1 cup (240 g) mayonnaise; 1 tablespoon (2 g) each minced fresh tarragon, chives, and parsley; 1 teaspoon anchovy paste, 1 teaspoon Dijon mustard, and the grated zest of 1 lemon.

Prosciutto-Wrapped Asparagus

This is a simple, elegant appetizer that's perfect for any occasion. The saltiness of the prosciutto complements the tender-crisp asparagus beautifully.

MAKES 4 SERVINGS

1 bunch asparagus (about 1 pound [450 g]), ends trimmed

2 tablespoons (30 ml) olive oil

Salt and freshly ground pepper

8 slices prosciutto

Preheat the oven to 400°F (200°C).

In a bowl, toss the trimmed asparagus with the olive oil and season with salt and pepper until evenly coated. Take a slice of prosciutto and wrap it around 3 or 4 asparagus stalks, starting from the bottom and working your way up. Repeat with the remaining prosciutto and asparagus. Place the bundles on a baking sheet.

Bake for 15 minutes, or until the prosciutto is crispy and the asparagus is tender.

Serve immediately.

CHUCK'S TIP

I would rather eat my asparagus served on toast with copious quantities of melted clarified butter, which falls into the toast along with the vegetable's essence. If you can bear to wait, garnish each portion with sieved hard-boiled egg white and crossed strips of pimiento.

Stuffed Mushrooms

Spanish serrano ham undergoes the same salt-curing and air-drying process as its renowned Italian counterpart, prosciutto. Produced mainly in western Spain, it ranks among the country's quintessential tapas selections. Typically sliced thicker than prosciutto, serrano offers a similar yet more robust, earthy taste—partly attributed to the acorns that feature prominently in the pigs' diet. While less common than prosciutto, serrano ham is increasingly found in delicatessens and gourmet food shops.

MAKES 12 SERVINGS

- 42 fresh cremini or white button mushrooms, each 2 to 3 inches (5 to 7.5 cm) in diameter, brushed clean
- 2 tablespoons (15 g) fresh breadcrumbs (see Note, page 96)
- 2 tablespoons (6 g) chopped fresh flat-leaf parsley
- 1 teaspoon minced fresh sage
- 1 large garlic clove, finely chopped
- 3 ounces (90 g) serrano ham or prosciutto, finely chopped
- 3 tablespoons (45 g) crème fraîche or sour cream, or as needed
- ½ teaspoon salt
- ¼ teaspoon freshly ground pepper
- 2 tablespoons (30 ml) dry white wine or vermouth
- 2 tablespoons (12 g) grated Parmigiano-Reggiano cheese, plus more for garnish

Preheat the oven to 400°F (200°C). Lightly oil one or two heavy baking dishes large enough to accommodate the mushrooms snugly in a single layer.

Trim off the rough base of each mushroom stem, then remove the stems and chop finely. In a large bowl, combine the chopped stems, breadcrumbs, parsley, sage, garlic, ham, crème fraîche, salt, and pepper. Mix together thoroughly. The mixture should hold together in clumps. If it seems dry, mix in another 1 to 2 teaspoons of crème fraîche.

Put the mushroom caps, stem sides up, in a steamer basket set over simmering water. Cover and steam until tender and glossy, about 3 minutes. Lift out the basket, allowing any moisture to drain, and let cool.

Spoon 1 generous teaspoon of the ham mixture onto the stem side of each mushroom cap and smooth it into an even, rounded mound. Place the mushrooms, stuffing side up, in the prepared baking dish(es). Drizzle the wine around the edges of the dish and sprinkle each cap with about ⅛ teaspoon of the cheese.

Bake, uncovered, until golden, about 30 minutes. Let cool for 5 minutes, garnish with more cheese, and serve warm or at room temperature.

MAKE-AHEAD TIP

The steamed mushrooms and stuffing can be stored separately in the refrigerator for up to 24 hours before stuffing.

Agaricus bisporus

Button vs. Cremini vs. Portobello

If you've ever stood in the produce aisle debating between white button mushrooms, portobellos, and brown creminis, here's the twist: They're all the same mushroom. White buttons, creminis, and portobellos are just *Agaricus bisporus* harvested at three different ages, which is why they taste and cook so differently. Understanding these stages lets you control the texture and depth of flavor in your cooking:

White Button—The Infancy Stage

These are the youngest and most widely cultivated mushrooms in the world. Harvested early, before their caps fully open, they possess a mild, subtle flavor and a firm, crisp texture. They soak up whatever you cook them with, so they're great in salads, quick sautés, and light sauces.

Cremini or "Baby Bella"—The Adolescence Stage

Creminis are simply white button mushrooms that have been allowed to age just a little longer. This maturation causes the skin to turn brown, while the water content inside evaporates slightly. The result is a denser, meatier texture and a significantly deeper, earthier flavor. They add a rustic note to stews and risottos, and work well in stuffings such as the one seen in this recipe, with serrano ham and crème fraîche.

Portobello—The Mature Stage

When a cremini is left to grow to its full size, it becomes a portobello. At this final stage, the cap expands entirely, exposing the dark gills underneath. Because so much moisture has naturally evaporated during growth, the portobello possesses an intensely concentrated, savory umami flavor and a thick, steak-like texture that makes it an excellent plant-based option for grilling or roasting.

Phyllo Cups with Caviar and Crème Fraîche

These elegant phyllo cups are perfect for holiday get-togethers. Filled with crème fraîche and topped with caviar, they look fanciful but are surprisingly easy to make. Simply stack buttered sheets of phyllo dough, cut them into squares, and bake them in a mini muffin pan. The cups can be made and cooled in advance, then filled just before guests arrive. While the recipe only calls for three sheets of dough, use six to have extra on hand in case some dry out.

MAKES 24 PHYLLO CUPS, 8 TO 12 SERVINGS

- 6 sheets phyllo dough, thawed
- 6 tablespoons (90 g) unsalted butter, melted and cooled slightly
- 6 ounces (180 g) crème fraîche
- 4 ounces (120 g) caviar
- 3 tablespoons (6 g) chopped fresh chives

Preheat the oven to 425°F (220°C). Lightly spray a 24-well mini muffin pan with nonstick cooking spray.

Place 1 phyllo sheet on a work surface and brush lightly with some of the melted butter, then place a second phyllo sheet on top. Repeat with a third sheet to create a total of 3 stacked sheets.

Using a pizza wheel, a pastry cutter, or a sharp knife, cut the stacked sheets into 2-inch (5 cm) squares. Press the squares into the prepared muffin wells, pressing them tightly into the shape of the well and overlapping the edges as needed.

Bake until the phyllo cups are golden brown and crisp, about 10 minutes. Transfer the pan to a wire rack and let the cups cool completely, then use an offset spatula to pop them out of the wells. Place the cups on a serving platter or plate.

Put the crème fraîche into a pastry bag and snip off a ⅛-inch (3 mm) opening. Pipe the crème fraîche into the cups. Top each with a bit of caviar and sprinkle with the chives.

Savory Puff Pastry Straws

Perfect to pair with wine or bubbly, these savory appetizers are simple to make using store-bought puff pastry. Keep a box in your freezer so you can whip up these twists at a moment's notice. Choose one of the toppings from the suggested list below; the quantities are for a single batch.

MAKES 16 STRAWS

STRAWS

All-purpose flour, for dusting

1 sheet frozen puff pastry, thawed

1 egg plus 1 teaspoon water, lightly beaten

Kosher salt

TOPPING (CHOOSE ONE)

3 tablespoons (21 g) poppy seeds

2 tablespoons (6 g) herbes de Provence

1½ tablespoons (9 g) smoked paprika

1 cup (100 g) lightly packed grated Parmesan cheese

Position one rack in the upper third and one rack in the lower third of the oven and preheat to 400°F (200°C). Line two baking sheets with Silpat baking mats or parchment paper.

On a lightly floured work surface, roll out the puff pastry into a 16-by-10-inch (41 by 25 cm) rectangle, with a long side facing you. Brush the entire surface of the pastry lightly with the egg mixture, then sprinkle the desired topping over the surface and press down slightly. Sprinkle lightly with salt. Using a lightly floured sharp knife or pastry cutter, cut the pastry lengthwise into strips 1 inch (2.5 cm) wide.

Working with one pastry strip at a time, start in the middle and twist the strip in the opposite direction three times on each side to form a spiral. Transfer to a prepared baking sheet and press the ends of the pastry into the Silpat mat to prevent it from unraveling while baking. Repeat with the remaining pastry strips, spacing them 1 inch (2.5 cm) apart. Place in the freezer for 15 minutes.

Bake until the pastries are deep golden brown and puffed up, 14 to 17 minutes. Let the pastries cool on the baking sheets for 5 minutes, then serve warm or at room temperature.

CHUCK'S TIP

Herbes de Provence is a traditional blend of herbs from the south of France. To make your own, for about ¼ cup (16 g), stir together 2 tablespoons (5 g) each of dried thyme, dried summer savory, and dried basil; 1 teaspoon whole fennel seeds; and ½ teaspoon dried culinary lavender. Store in an airtight container.

Shrimp Cocktail with Spicy Horseradish

This classic appetizer features perfectly cooked shrimp paired with a zesty horseradish cocktail sauce that delivers just the right amount of heat. Based on Williams Sonoma's spicy cocktail sauce, this recipe creates an elegant starter that's perfect for entertaining.

MAKES 6 TO 8 SERVINGS

SPICY HORSERADISH COCKTAIL SAUCE

1 cup (240 ml) ketchup or chili sauce

2 to 3 tablespoons (30 to 45 g) prepared horseradish (adjust to taste)

Finely grated zest of 1 lemon

1 tablespoon (15 ml) fresh lemon juice

1 teaspoon Worcestershire sauce

Hot pepper sauce

Pinch of kosher salt

SHRIMP

2 bay leaves

1 lemon, halved

2 teaspoons kosher salt

1 teaspoon whole black peppercorns

1 teaspoon Old Bay seasoning

2 pounds (900 g) large shrimp (26 to 30 count), peeled and deveined, tails on

Lemon wedges, for serving (optional)

Fresh parsley, for garnish (optional)

To make the spicy horseradish cocktail sauce: In a small bowl, stir together the ketchup, horseradish, lemon zest, lemon juice, and Worcestershire sauce. Season with hot pepper sauce and salt to taste. Cover and refrigerate for at least 30 minutes to allow the flavors to meld.

To make the shrimp: Fill a large pot with water and add the bay leaves, the juice from both lemon halves (drop the rinds in too), salt, peppercorns, and Old Bay seasoning. Bring to a rolling boil, then add the shrimp. Cook just until the shrimp turn pink and curl slightly, 2 to 3 minutes. Don't overcook. Immediately drain and plunge the shrimp into an ice water bath to stop the cooking. Once completely cooled, drain and pat dry. Refrigerate until ready to serve.

To serve, arrange the chilled shrimp on a platter around small bowls of the cocktail sauce. Garnish with lemon wedges and fresh parsley if desired. Provide small spoons for the sauce.

Deviled Eggs Three Ways

This is an elegant take on the classic appetizer, offering three sophisticated variations. Perfect for entertaining, these deviled eggs transform a simple party staple into something special.

MAKES 36 PIECES (12 PER VARIATION)

18 large eggs (6 per variation)

CLASSIC WITH SWEET PICKLES

6 egg yolks (from base recipe above)

2 tablespoons (30 g) mayonnaise

1 teaspoon Dijon mustard

1 tablespoon (6 g) finely chopped sweet pickle

Salt and freshly ground pepper

Sweet paprika, for garnish

GOURMET WITH LEMON, CHIVES, AND CAPERS

6 egg yolks (from base recipe above)

1 tablespoon (15 g) Dijon mustard

1 tablespoon (15 g) mayonnaise

½ teaspoon salt

½ teaspoon freshly ground pepper

2 tablespoons (4 g) minced fresh chives, plus more for garnish

1 teaspoon minced shallot

1½ tablespoons (12 g) capers, rinsed, drained, and coarsely chopped

2 teaspoons grated lemon zest

Place the eggs in a large saucepan and cover with cold water by 1 to 1½ inches (2.5 to 4 cm). Bring to a boil over medium-high heat. When the water reaches a boil, remove from the heat, cover, and let stand for 20 minutes. Transfer the eggs to an ice water bath using a slotted spoon.

Let cool for 5 minutes, then peel under cold running water. Cut the eggs in half lengthwise and carefully remove the yolks. Set whites aside.

To make the classic with sweet pickles: In a small bowl, mash the egg yolks with the mayonnaise and mustard until smooth and fluffy. Fold in the chopped sweet pickle. Season with salt and pepper. Spoon the mixture into 12 egg white halves, mounding slightly. Sprinkle with sweet paprika.

To make the gourmet with lemon, chives, and capers: In a small bowl, combine the egg yolks, mustard, mayonnaise, salt, pepper, chives, shallot, capers, and lemon zest. Using a fork, mash together until the yolk mixture is smooth and fluffy. Spoon the mixture into 12 egg white halves, mounding slightly. Garnish with additional fresh chives.

Continued on page 58

Continued from page 56

ELEVATED WITH CRISPY PROSCIUTTO

2 ounces (60 g) thinly sliced prosciutto

6 egg yolks (from base recipe above)

2 tablespoons (30 g) mayonnaise

1 teaspoon Dijon mustard

1 tablespoon (15 ml) fresh lemon juice

1 teaspoon minced fresh thyme

Salt and freshly ground pepper

Microgreens, for garnish (optional)

To make the elevated with crispy prosciutto: Preheat the oven to 375°F (190°C). Line a baking sheet with parchment paper.

Arrange the prosciutto in a single layer on the baking sheet. Bake until crispy, 8 to 10 minutes. Cool completely, then crumble into small pieces.

In a small bowl, mash the egg yolks with the mayonnaise, mustard, lemon juice, and thyme until smooth. Season with salt and pepper. Fold in half of the crispy prosciutto. Spoon the mixture into 12 egg white halves. Top with the remaining prosciutto and the microgreens, if desired.

Baked Brie en Croûte with Apple Compote

Flaky pastry, melted Brie, and spiced apple compote come together in this elegant make-ahead appetizer. Assemble it up to two weeks in advance, freeze, and bake straight from frozen when guests arrive—it's that easy!

MAKES 8 SERVINGS

1 tablespoon (12 g) unsalted butter

2 Golden Delicious apples, peeled, cored, and cut into ½-inch (13 mm) dice

¼ cup (50 g) sugar

⅛ teaspoon ground cardamom

1 round Brie cheese, 6 to 8 ounces (180 to 240 g) and about 4½ inches (11.5 cm) wide, slightly chilled

10-inch (25 cm) round puff pastry dough, rolled out to ¼ inch (6 mm) thick

1 egg, beaten with 1 tablespoon (15 ml) water

Plain water crackers, for serving

In a 2-quart (1.8 L) sauté pan over medium heat, melt the butter. Add the apples and sauté, stirring occasionally, until the apples are tender and have released most of their liquid, 5 to 7 minutes. Add the sugar and cardamom, stir to dissolve, and cook, stirring occasionally, until most of the liquid has evaporated, 12 to 15 minutes more. Remove from the heat and let the apple compote cool to room temperature.

Preheat the oven to 375°F (190°C). Line a baking sheet with parchment paper.

With a sharp knife, cut the cheese in half horizontally. On a clean work surface, place one half of the cheese, sliced side up, and evenly spread ½ cup (120 g) of the apple compote over it. Set the other half, sliced side down, over the compote and spread ½ cup (120 g) of compote over the top.

Place the dough on a lightly floured surface and set the cheese in the center of the dough. Fold the dough up over the sides of the cheese, pleating the upper edges to fit snugly around the cheese. Pinch the dough together in the center to seal. Brush the dough evenly with the egg wash and place on the prepared baking sheet.

Bake until the pastry is golden all over and crisp, 40 to 45 minutes. Let it rest for 5 minutes, then transfer to a platter along with a sharp knife and the crackers. Serve any remaining compote alongside.

NOTE

This appetizer offers excellent make-ahead convenience—prepare it up to 2 weeks before serving. Assemble the pastry with cheese and apple compote but skip the egg wash. Wrap the assembled pastry tightly in plastic wrap and freeze until needed. When ready to serve, brush the frozen pastry with egg wash and bake at 350°F (180°C) for 45 to 50 minutes.

Sautéed Figs with Slab Bacon

This simple combination of lightly cooked figs and crispy bacon is the perfect balance of sweet and salty and a great choice for holiday gatherings. Our test kitchen chefs recommend serving it with a creamy cheese like Gorgonzola or a triple crème Brie.

MAKES 20 PIECES, 5 TO 10 SERVINGS

3 slices thick-cut bacon, cut into 1-inch (2.5 cm) pieces

10 fresh figs, halved lengthwise

Extra-virgin olive oil, for drizzling

Honey or balsamic glaze, for drizzling

In a large sauté pan off the heat, arrange the bacon pieces in a single layer. Set the pan over medium-high heat and cook until the bacon is crispy, about 2 minutes, then turn the bacon and cook for 1 minute more. Transfer to a paper towel-lined plate. Pour off all but 1 to 2 tablespoons (15 to 30 ml) of the bacon fat from the pan.

Return the pan to medium-high heat and place the figs, cut sides down, in the pan. Cook until the figs are lightly charred and softened, about 1 minute. Turn the figs and cook just until they are slightly wilted on the outside, about 30 seconds more.

Transfer the figs, cut sides up, to a serving platter and top each with a piece of bacon. Add a drizzle of olive oil and honey and serve warm.

Baked Feta with Sumac Grapes and Green Olives

This easy, Greek-inspired recipe makes for an impressive appetizer. A whole block of feta is baked until wonderfully creamy, perfect for spreading on crusty bread or crackers. Red grapes roast alongside, becoming intensely sweet and caramelized, while green olives and a dash of sumac add briny and citrusy notes.

MAKES 4 TO 6 SERVINGS

One 7-ounce (210 g) block feta cheese, left whole

1½ cups (275 g) seedless red grapes, 1 cup (185 g) left whole and ½ cup (90 g) halved lengthwise

1 cup (155 g) green olives

⅓ cup (80 ml) extra-virgin olive oil

1 tablespoon (3 g) roughly chopped fresh oregano or tarragon, plus more for garnish

1 teaspoon ground sumac

1 teaspoon sesame seeds

Zest or peel from 1 lemon

Freshly ground pepper

Honey, for drizzling

Juice of ½ lemon

Flaky sea salt

Crusty French bread or crackers, for serving

Preheat the oven to 350°F (180°C).

Place the block of feta in the center of a 3-quart (2.7 L) casserole dish. Arrange the whole grapes around the cheese, followed by the halved grapes and the olives. Drizzle all over with the olive oil, then sprinkle with the oregano, sumac, sesame seeds, half of the lemon zest, and several grindings of pepper.

Cover the dish and bake for 10 minutes, then uncover the dish and bake for 10 minutes more. Leave the dish in the oven and increase the oven to broil. Broil until the feta is soft and just browned and the whole grapes are burst and caramelized; start checking after 2 minutes of broiling, then continue to cook longer as needed.

Carefully remove the dish from the oven and let cool slightly. Drizzle with honey and garnish with the remaining lemon zest, oregano, lemon juice, and flaky sea salt. Serve with crusty bread or crackers.

LE CREUSET

Gougères

These light, savory cheese puffs are a staple of French entertaining. With their crisp, golden-brown exterior and soft, hollow, cheesy interior, they're perfect served warm as an appetizer.

MAKES 20 TO 25 PUFFS

½ cup (120) whole milk

½ cup (120) water

½ cup (115 g) unsalted butter, cut into small pieces

1 teaspoon salt

1 cup (140 g) all-purpose flour

4 large eggs

1½ cups (170 g) grated Gruyère cheese

Preheat the oven to 400°F (200°C). Line a baking sheet with parchment paper.

In a heavy-bottomed saucepan over medium-high heat, bring the milk, water, butter, and salt to a rolling boil. Remove the pan from the heat and add the flour all at once, stirring vigorously with a wooden spoon until the mixture comes together and pulls away from the sides of the pan.

Return the pan to the heat and stir constantly for about 1 minute to cook off excess moisture. The dough should form a smooth ball.

Transfer the dough to a large bowl and let it cool slightly for a few minutes. Add the eggs one at a time, mixing well after each addition. The dough will look lumpy and separated at first, but it will become smooth and glossy after each egg is fully incorporated.

Reserve about 2 tablespoons (12 g) of the grated cheese for topping and fold the rest into the dough until it's evenly distributed.

Using two spoons or a piping bag, drop rounded tablespoons of the dough onto the prepared baking sheet, spacing them about 1½ inches (4 cm) apart. Sprinkle the remaining grated cheese over the top of each puff.

Bake for 20 to 25 minutes, or until the gougères are puffed, golden brown, and firm to the touch.

Let them cool for a few minutes on the baking sheet before serving them warm.

Chicken Satay Skewers with Peanut Sauce

Curry powder is a blend of up to twenty spices, including turmeric, which gives it its distinctive yellow color. Common ingredients are cumin, curry leaves, cardamom, coriander, fennel, mustard seeds, mace, fenugreek, and red and black pepper. The Madras curry powder used in this recipe is a hotter blend popular in southern India.

MAKES 12 TO 16 SKEWERS, 4 TO 8 SERVINGS

1½ pounds (680 g) boneless, skinless chicken thighs

½ cup (120 ml) coconut milk

¼ cup (60 ml) fish sauce

3 tablespoons (40 g) firmly packed light brown sugar

2 tablespoons (6 g) chopped fresh cilantro

1 tablespoon (6 g) Madras curry powder

1 tablespoon (15 ml) canola oil

Peanut sauce, for serving

Cut the chicken into strips 4 inches (10 cm) long by ½ inch (13 mm) wide. In a large bowl, stir together the coconut milk, fish sauce, brown sugar, cilantro, and curry powder. Add the chicken and stir until evenly coated. Cover and refrigerate for at least 1 hour or up to overnight.

Preheat an indoor electric grill to medium-high heat according to the manufacturer's instructions.

Remove the chicken from the marinade and discard the marinade. Using 12 to 16 wooden skewers, each 9 inches (23 cm) long, thread 2 or 3 pieces of chicken onto each skewer. Brush the grill with the oil. Arrange the skewers on the grill and cook until the chicken is golden brown on both sides, about 10 minutes total. Transfer the skewers to a warmed platter. Pour the peanut sauce into a small bowl and serve alongside.

The Comfort of Home Cooking

3reakfast, Soups, Stews, Casseroles, and Pasta

omfort food isn't about complexity or exotic ingredients. It's about the perfect marriage of echnique and heart, transforming simple, honest ingredients into dishes that feel like home. Vhether it's the gentle bubble of French Onion Soup (page 85) as the cheese melts into olden perfection, the satisfying richness of Classic Macaroni and Cheese (page 96) that tastes ven better than you remembered, or the Sunday morning luxury of Classic Eggs Benedict page 77), these are the recipes that anchor our most cherished food memories.

Roman-Style Meatballs with Gnocchi alla Romana

These robust Roman meatballs combine ground beef, pork, and prosciutto pieces, then are simmered in rich tomato sauce. The secret to tender meatballs lies in gentle handling—mix the ingredients just until combined to avoid a dense texture.

MAKES 6 TO 8 SERVINGS

- 1½ cups (175 g) fresh breadcrumbs (see Note, page 96)
- ½ cup (120 ml) milk
- 4 ounces (120 g) finely chopped prosciutto
- 1 pound (450 g) ground beef
- 1 pound (450 g) ground pork
- 2 eggs, lightly beaten
- ½ cup (50 g) grated Parmigiano-Reggiano cheese
- 2 tablespoons (8 g) finely chopped fresh flat-leaf parsley
- 2 teaspoons finely chopped fresh oregano
- 6 tablespoons (24 g) finely chopped fresh basil
- 5 garlic cloves, minced
- 1 teaspoon kosher salt, plus more as needed
- ½ teaspoon freshly ground pepper, plus more as needed
- 5 tablespoons (75 ml) olive oil
- 1 yellow onion, diced
- One 28-ounce (840 g) can crushed tomatoes with juices
- 1 recipe Gnocchi alla Romana (page 76), for serving

In a small bowl, combine the breadcrumbs and milk and let stand for 10 minutes.

In a large bowl, combine the prosciutto, beef, pork, eggs, cheese, parsley, oregano, 3 tablespoons (12 g) of the basil, 3 of the minced garlic cloves, salt, and pepper. Add the soaked breadcrumbs and mix gently until combined. Divide the meat mixture into ¼-cup (60 g) portions and roll into balls. Place on a parchment-lined baking sheet.

In an 11-inch (28 cm) French skillet over medium-high heat, warm 2 tablespoons (30 ml) of the olive oil. Working in two batches, brown the meatballs on all sides, about 8 minutes per batch. Transfer to a plate.

In the same pan over medium heat, warm the remaining 3 tablespoons (45 ml) of olive oil. Add the onion and cook, stirring occasionally, until softened and translucent, about 8 minutes. Add the remaining 2 minced garlic cloves and cook for 1 minute. Add the tomatoes and their juices and season with salt and pepper. Bring to a simmer and cook until the sauce thickens, about 20 minutes. Stir in the remaining 3 tablespoons (12 g) of basil.

Add the meatballs to the pan and cook, turning occasionally and basting with the sauce, until cooked through, about 30 minutes. Transfer to a platter and serve immediately with the gnocchi alongside.

Bacon and Leek Quiche

Few dishes are as versatile for brunch as quiche. Its rich egg custard nestled in a buttery crust can take on endless combinations of herbs, meats, cheeses, and vegetables. Delicious hot or at room temperature, quiche is a smart choice when you're serving a variety of dishes.

MAKES 6 SERVINGS

1 recipe Basic Pie Dough, for a single-crust pie (page 72)

4 thick slices applewood-smoked bacon, coarsely chopped

1 tablespoon (15 g) unsalted butter

2 small leeks, white and pale green parts, washed well and chopped

1 cup (240 ml) half-and-half

2 large eggs

½ teaspoon kosher salt

¼ teaspoon freshly ground pepper

⅛ teaspoon freshly grated nutmeg

1 cup (140 g) shredded Gruyère cheese

Place the dough on a lightly floured work surface and dust the top with flour. (If the dough is chilled hard, let it stand at room temperature for a few minutes until it begins to soften before rolling it out.) Roll out into a round about 12 inches (30.5 cm) in diameter and about ⅛ inch (3 mm) thick. Transfer to a 9-inch (23 cm) tart pan with a removable bottom, gently fitting the dough into the bottom and sides of the pan. Using scissors or a small knife, trim the dough, leaving a ½-inch (13 mm) overhang. Fold the overhanging dough over and into the pan, pressing it firmly against the dough on the sides of the pan; the dough should be doubly thick at the sides and rise about ⅛ inch (3 mm) above the pan rim. Line the dough with a piece of aluminum foil and freeze for 30 minutes.

Position a rack in the lower third of the oven and preheat to 375°F (190°C).

Place the dough-lined pan on a baking sheet and fill the foil with pie weights or dried beans. Bake until the dough is set and beginning to brown, about 20 minutes.

Meanwhile, in a frying pan, fry the bacon over medium heat, stirring, until crisp and golden, about 6 minutes. Using a slotted spoon, transfer to paper towels to drain. Pour out the fat and wipe the pan clean with paper towels. Add the butter to the pan and melt over medium heat. Add the leeks and cook, stirring occasionally, until tender, about 10 minutes. Transfer to a plate and let cool slightly.

Continued on page 72

Continued from page 71

Remove the baking sheet with the tart pan from the oven. Remove the foil and weights.

In a bowl, whisk together the half-and-half, eggs, salt, pepper, and nutmeg until combined. Scatter the leeks, bacon, and Gruyère evenly in the pastry shell. Carefully pour the egg mixture into the shell. Return to the oven and bake until the filling is puffed and golden brown, about 30 minutes. Let cool slightly, then serve.

Basic Pie Dough

MAKES ONE 9-INCH PIE CRUST

1⅓ cups all-purpose flour
1 tablespoon (12 g) sugar
¼ teaspoon salt
½ cup (120 g) cold unsalted butter, cubed
¼ cup (60 ml) ice water, plus more as needed

Fit a food processor with the metal blade. Add the flour, sugar, and salt and pulse two or three times. Add the cold butter cubes and pulse eight to ten times until pea-size pieces remain. Add the ice water and pulse ten to twelve times. If the dough crumbles when pinched, add more water, 1 tablespoon (15 ml) at a time, until it holds together. Transfer to a floured surface, shape into 6-inch (15 cm) disk, wrap in plastic, and refrigerate for at least 1 hour.

Blueberry Buttermilk Pancakes

Make these pancakes when blueberries are at their peak, from late spring through late summer. When mixing the batter, stir gently—overmixing develops the gluten in the flour and can lead to tough pancakes.

MAKES 16 PANCAKES, 4 SERVINGS

2 eggs

2 cups (280 g) all-purpose flour, sifted

3 tablespoons (36 g) granulated sugar

2 teaspoons baking powder

1 teaspoon baking soda

1 teaspoon salt

2¼ cups (540 ml) buttermilk

4 tablespoons (60 g) unsalted butter, melted

½ teaspoon vanilla extract

1 to 2 tablespoons (15 to 30 ml) vegetable oil or nonstick cooking spray

1 cup (145 g) fresh blueberries

Confectioners' sugar, for dusting

Softened butter, for serving

Warm maple syrup, for serving

Preheat the oven to 200°F (95°C).

In a bowl, using an electric mixer, beat the eggs on medium speed until frothy. Add the flour, granulated sugar, baking powder, baking soda, salt, buttermilk, melted butter, and vanilla. Stir just until the batter is smooth and no lumps of flour remain; do not overmix.

Heat an electric griddle to medium-high heat until a few drops of water flicked onto the surface skitter across it. Lightly grease the griddle with oil or spray with nonstick cooking spray. Using a batter dispenser set on the large setting, dispense the batter onto the griddle. Alternatively, ladle about ⅓ cup (80 g) of batter onto the griddle for each pancake. Scatter 1 tablespoon (9 g) of blueberries evenly over each pancake. Cook until bubbles form on top and the batter is set, 1 to 2 minutes. Using a spatula, flip the pancakes and cook until golden brown on the other side, 2 to 3 minutes. Transfer to a baking sheet and keep warm in the oven while cooking the remaining pancakes.

Dust the pancakes with confectioners' sugar and serve warm with butter and maple syrup.

Grilled Cheese with Creamy Tomato Soup

For many Americans, childhood comfort food meant grilled cheese sandwiches and canned tomato soup. This version elevates that beloved pairing with tangy cheddar melted between slices of sourdough or pain au levain and a soup made from slow-roasted tomatoes—turning a simple memory into a rich, grown-up treat.

MAKES 4 SERVINGS

CREAMY TOMATO SOUP

4 pounds (1.8 kg) plum tomatoes

2 tablespoons (30 ml) olive oil

1 tablespoon (15 g) unsalted butter

2 celery stalks, finely chopped

⅓ cup (40 g) finely chopped shallots

½ cup (120 ml) chicken stock or broth, or as needed

1 teaspoon fresh thyme leaves

½ teaspoon sugar

½ cup (120 ml) heavy cream

Kosher salt and freshly ground pepper

GRILLED CHEESE

12 ounces (360 g) mild cheddar cheese, thinly sliced

8 slices sourdough bread or pain au levain

4 tablespoons (60 g) unsalted butter, at room temperature

To make the soup: Preheat the oven to 400°F (200°C). Lightly oil a rimmed baking sheet.

Cut the tomatoes in half lengthwise. Place them, cut sides up, on the prepared baking sheet and brush with the oil. Roast until the tomatoes look somewhat shriveled, about 45 minutes. Let cool for about 20 minutes. Transfer the tomatoes and any juices to a food processor. Pulse until chopped, then rub the tomatoes and their juices through a coarse-mesh sieve placed over a bowl. You should have about 3½ cups (840 g) of tomato purée. Discard the contents of the sieve.

In a large saucepan, melt the butter over medium-low heat. Add the celery and cook, stirring occasionally, until tender, about 5 minutes. Add the shallots and cook, stirring occasionally, until softened, about 3 minutes. Stir in the tomato purée, stock, and thyme and bring to a simmer over medium-high heat. Decrease the heat to medium-low and simmer, uncovered, for about 15 minutes. Stir in the sugar. In three or four batches, transfer the soup to a blender and process until smooth. Transfer to a clean saucepan, add the cream, and heat until piping hot but not boiling. If the soup seems thick, thin with more stock. Season to taste with salt and pepper.

To make the grilled cheese sandwiches: Heat a griddle or two large frying pans over medium heat until hot.

For each sandwich, place one-fourth of the cheese on top of a bread slice and top with a second bread slice. Spread the outsides of each sandwich with 1 tablespoon (15 g) of the butter. Place on the griddle, decrease the heat to medium-low, and cook until the undersides are golden brown, 3 to 4 minutes. Flip the sandwiches and brown the other side, 3 to 4 minutes more.

Ladle the soup into warmed bowls. Serve at once, with the hot sandwiches alongside.

Gnocchi alla Romana

These delicate Roman-style gnocchi feature semolina flour enriched with milk, butter, egg yolks, and Parmigiano-Reggiano cheese. The dough is shaped into disks, layered in a baking dish, and baked until golden.

MAKES 8 SERVINGS

5½ cups (1.3 L) milk

2 cups (280 g) semolina

2 teaspoons kosher salt

1¼ cups (125 g) grated Parmigiano-Reggiano cheese

2 egg yolks

6 tablespoons (90 g) unsalted butter, cut into small cubes, plus 3 tablespoons (45 ml) melted butter

In a 4-quart (3.6 L) saucepan over medium-high heat, bring the milk to a simmer. Add the semolina in a thin, steady stream, whisking constantly until incorporated. Decrease the heat to medium-low, add the salt, and continue whisking to prevent lumps from forming. Cook, stirring and scraping the bottom and sides of the pan, until the semolina is thick and starts to pull away from the sides of the pan, about 10 minutes. Remove from the heat and stir in ¾ cup (75 g) of the cheese, the egg yolks, and the 6 tablespoons (90 g) butter until incorporated.

Spray a 9-by-13-inch (23 by 33 cm) pan with nonstick cooking spray, line the bottom with parchment paper, and spray again. Pour the semolina mixture into the pan, spreading it evenly and smoothing the top with a rubber spatula. Cover and refrigerate until firm, about 2 hours.

Preheat the oven to 425°F (220°C). Butter a 9-inch (23 cm) French skillet.

Using a 2½-inch (6.5 cm) biscuit cutter, cut the gnocchi into rounds. Arrange the gnocchi in the pan so they are overlapping, resembling shingles. Brush the top of the gnocchi with the 3 tablespoons (45 ml) of melted butter and sprinkle with the remaining ½ cup (50 g) of cheese. Transfer the pan to the oven and bake until the top is golden brown, 30 to 35 minutes. Let rest for 10 minutes, then serve immediately.

Classic Eggs Benedict

This timeless brunch classic is always in style. When tomatoes are at their peak, elevate the dish by adding a broiled tomato slice on top of the ham before you crown it with the egg and silky hollandaise sauce.

MAKES 4 SERVINGS

HOLLANDAISE SAUCE

4 egg yolks

2 tablespoons (30 ml) lemon juice

1 tablespoon (15 ml) water

⅛ teaspoon salt

2 pinches freshly ground white pepper

Pinch of cayenne pepper

1 cup (240 g) unsalted butter, melted and cooled slightly

BENEDICTS

4 English muffins, split, or 8 crumpets

3 tablespoons (45 g) softened unsalted butter

8 slices baked ham, each ¼ inch (6 mm) thick and cut to fit English muffins or crumpets

8 eggs

Preheat the broiler.

To make the hollandaise sauce: In a small, heavy saucepan over low heat, whisk the egg yolks, lemon juice, and water constantly until the mixture begins to thicken. Remove from the heat and continue whisking for about 1 minute more. Transfer the mixture to a blender, add the salt, white pepper, and cayenne pepper, and blend until smooth. Let cool for 1 minute. With the motor running, slowly pour in the melted butter in a thin stream until incorporated. Taste and adjust the seasonings. Transfer the sauce to a saucepan and keep warm over very low heat.

To make the benedicts: Lightly spread the cut sides of each muffin or the top of each crumpet with 1 teaspoon of the butter and broil until golden, 3 to 5 minutes. Turn off the broiler, cover the muffins or crumpets with aluminum foil, and keep warm in the oven.

Meanwhile, in a small sauté pan over medium-high heat, melt the remaining 1 teaspoon of butter. Add the ham and cook until golden, about 2 minutes per side. Keep warm.

Fill an egg-poaching pan with ½ inch (13 mm) of water, set the pan over medium heat, and bring to a simmer. Lightly coat the poaching cups with nonstick cooking spray and crack an egg into each cup. Cover and cook until the whites are firm and the yolks are glazed over but still soft, about 3 minutes, or until done to your liking. Transfer the eggs to a warmed plate and repeat with the remaining eggs.

Place 2 muffin halves or 2 crumpets on each of four warmed individual plates. Top each muffin half or crumpet with a slice of ham, an egg, and some of the sauce. Serve immediately.

Lobster and Corn Chowder

A staple of New England cooking, lobster chowder calls to mind carefree summers by the shore. Make it during peak season, when lobster and fresh corn are at their best.

MAKES 6 SERVINGS

- 2 live lobsters, each 1¼ to 1½ pounds (567 to 680 g)
- 1 tablespoon (15 ml) canola oil
- 5 cups (1.2 L) low-sodium chicken stock
- ½ cup (120 ml) white wine
- 3 ears corn, kernels removed, kernels and corncobs reserved
- 3 slices bacon, diced
- 1 yellow onion, chopped
- 2 large carrots, diced
- 3 celery stalks, diced
- 2 cups (473 ml) heavy cream
- 4 Yukon gold potatoes, cut into ½-inch (13 mm) pieces
- Salt and freshly ground pepper
- 1 teaspoon chopped fresh thyme
- 2 teaspoons chopped fresh chives

Bring a large pot three-fourths full of salted water to a boil over high heat. Add the lobsters one at a time, headfirst. Cover and cook until the lobsters are red, about 7 minutes. Transfer the lobsters to a large bowl filled with ice water and let cool completely. Remove the meat from the claws, knuckles, and tails. Reserve the shells and bodies and refrigerate the meat until ready to use.

In a large pot over high heat, warm the oil. Add the reserved lobster shells and bodies and sauté until lightly browned, about 5 minutes. Add the stock, wine, and corncobs, bring to a simmer, and cook until reduced to about 2½ cups (600 ml), 25 to 30 minutes.

In a Dutch oven over medium heat, sauté the bacon, stirring occasionally, until crispy and browned, 3 to 4 minutes. Add the onion, carrots, celery, and corn kernels and sauté, stirring occasionally, until tender, 4 to 5 minutes. Strain the lobster-corn stock into the Dutch oven, add the cream, and bring to a simmer. Stir in the potatoes, return to a simmer, and decrease the heat to medium-low. Cook until the potatoes are tender, 15 to 18 minutes. Stir in the lobster meat, salt, pepper, thyme, and chives. Cook, stirring occasionally, until the lobster is heated through, 2 to 3 minutes. Taste and adjust the seasonings.

Ladle the chowder into warmed soup bowls and serve immediately.

Butternut Squash Soup with Hazelnut Gremolata

Golden, crisp croutons bring crunch to this velvety butternut squash soup, while an Italian-style gremolata made with toasted hazelnuts adds brightness and freshness. Perfect for a cozy autumn lunch, the soup also makes an elegant first course for a Thanksgiving meal. The soup, croutons, and gremolata can all be prepared up to 2 days ahead (simply reheat the soup gently in a saucepan) but wait to combine them until just before serving.

MAKES 8 SERVINGS

CROUTONS

1 small loaf crusty sourdough bread, about 12 ounces (360 g), torn into 1-inch (2.5 cm) pieces

½ cup (120 g) unsalted butter

⅛ teaspoon kosher salt, plus more if needed

Preheat the oven to 325°F (170°C).

To make the croutons: Place the bread in a large bowl. In a small fry pan over medium heat, melt the butter. Decrease the heat to medium-low and cook, stirring frequently, until the butter is toasty brown and smells nutty, about 5 minutes, watching the butter carefully at the end to prevent it from burning. Pour the butter over the bread and stir until evenly coated. Season with the salt.

Spread the bread in a single layer on a baking sheet and bake until the croutons are light golden brown, about 20 minutes, tossing the bread pieces once halfway through the baking time. The croutons should be crisp on the edges but still give a little when pinched with your fingers. Taste and season with more salt if desired. Set aside. (The croutons can be stored, covered, at room temperature for up to 2 days.)

Increase the oven temperature to 400°F (200°C).

Continued on page 82

Continued from page 80

SOUP

2 large butternut squashes, each 1½ to 2 pounds (675 to 910 g)

6 tablespoons (90 g) unsalted butter

2 yellow onions, chopped

4 fresh sage leaves, chopped, plus more leaves for garnish (optional)

6 cups (1.5 L) chicken or vegetable broth

Kosher salt and freshly ground pepper

Pinch of ground nutmeg (optional)

Pinch of sugar (optional)

GREMOLATA

⅓ cup (60 g) chopped toasted hazelnuts

1 cup (30 g) fresh flat-leaf parsley leaves

Grated zest and juice of 1 lemon

2 garlic cloves, minced

Extra-virgin olive oil, as needed

Kosher salt

To make the soup: Prick each squash several times with the tip of a knife. Place the whole squashes on a baking sheet and roast until they feel somewhat soft to the touch and a knife penetrates the skin easily, about 1 hour. Remove from the oven and, when cool enough to handle, cut in half lengthwise and remove and discard the seeds and fibers. Scoop out the pulp into a bowl and set aside.

While the squash is roasting, make the gremolata: In a food processor, combine the hazelnuts, parsley, lemon zest, and garlic. Pulse until the hazelnuts are about the size of sunflower seeds, the parsley is minced, and the mixture is just combined. Transfer to a bowl. Stir in the lemon juice and enough olive oil to make a thick sauce. Season with salt. Set aside, or cover and refrigerate until ready to use, up to 2 days.

To finish the soup: In a saucepan over low heat, melt the butter. Add the onions and chopped sage and cook, stirring occasionally, until the onions are tender and translucent, 8 to 10 minutes. Add the broth and squash pulp, increase the heat to high, and bring to a boil. Decrease the heat to low and simmer for a few minutes to combine the flavors. Remove from the heat.

Working in batches, purée the soup in a blender or food processor. Return to a clean saucepan. Alternatively, pass the soup through a food mill placed over the pan. Reheat gently over medium-low heat. Season with salt and pepper. Taste the soup and add the nutmeg and sugar if a little more sweetness is desired.

Ladle the soup into warmed bowls and top with the croutons and gremolata, dividing them evenly. Garnish with additional sage leaves, if desired, and serve immediately.

The Coziest Chicken Noodle Soup

Nothing says comfort quite like a steaming bowl of homemade chicken noodle soup. This classic recipe delivers cozy, nourishing goodness in every spoonful, thanks to a hearty medley of fresh vegetables, tender shredded chicken, and comforting egg noodles simmered in flavorful broth. Perfect for chilly evenings, under-the-weather days, or simply when you crave a taste of home, this soup is proof that simple ingredients—prepared with care—can yield the coziest of meals. Serve with a sprinkle of fresh parsley and savor the warmth.

MAKES 4 TO 6 SERVINGS

2 tablespoons (30 ml) olive oil

2 stalks celery, finely chopped

1 leek, white part only, halved, rinsed well, and thinly sliced

1 carrot, finely chopped

5 cups (1.2 L) chicken stock, homemade or purchased

1 bay leaf

¼ teaspoon dried thyme

2 cups (280 g) shredded cooked chicken, homemade or purchased

8 ounces (240 g) dried egg noodles

Salt and freshly ground pepper

¼ cup (16 g) minced fresh flat-leaf parsley

In a large saucepan over medium heat, warm the olive oil. Add the celery, leek, and carrot and sauté until softened, about 5 minutes.

Pour in the chicken stock and add the bay leaf, thyme, and shredded chicken. Bring to a boil over medium-high heat. Add the noodles, stir well, and cook until just tender, about 10 minutes.

Remove and discard the bay leaf. Season with salt and pepper.

Ladle the soup into warmed bowls, garnish with the parsley, and serve immediately.

French Onion Soup

Silky onions, robust stock, and a blanket of nutty melted cheese—these essential elements give this classic soup its bold flavor and make it a cornerstone of French cuisine, beloved at American tables as well. Take the time to prepare your own stock and you'll be rewarded with rich depth and irresistible savory character.

MAKES 8 SERVINGS

2 tablespoons (30 g) unsalted butter

2½ pounds (1.1 kg) yellow onions, halved and thinly sliced

1 tablespoon (8 g) all-purpose flour

1 cup (240 ml) dry white wine

8 cups (1.9 L) beef stock

2 teaspoons minced fresh thyme or 1 teaspoon dried

1 bay leaf

Kosher salt and freshly ground pepper

1 crusty baguette

2⅔ cups (375 g) shredded Gruyère cheese

In a large, heavy sauté pan, melt the butter over medium heat. Add the onions, stir well, cover, and cook for 5 minutes. Uncover, decrease the heat to medium-low, and cook, stirring occasionally, until tender and deep golden brown, about 30 minutes.

Sprinkle the flour over the onions and stir until combined. Gradually stir in the wine, then the stock, and finally the thyme and bay leaf. Bring to a boil over high heat, decrease the heat to medium-low, and simmer, uncovered, until slightly reduced, about 30 minutes. Season with salt and pepper. Discard the bay leaf.

Meanwhile, preheat the broiler. Have ready eight 1½-cup (360 g) broiler-proof soup crocks. Cut the baguette into 16 slices, sizing them so that 2 slices will fit inside each crock. Arrange the bread slices on a baking sheet and broil, turning once, until lightly toasted on both sides, about 1 minute total. Set the slices aside. Position the oven rack about 12 inches (30.5 cm) from the heat source and leave the broiler on.

Ladle the hot soup into the crocks. Place 2 toasted bread slices, overlapping if necessary, on top of the soup and sprinkle each crock evenly with about ⅓ cup (45 g) of the Gruyère. Broil until the cheese is bubbling, about 2 minutes. Serve at once.

CHUCK'S TIP

A steaming bowl of cheese-topped onion soup makes a memorable post-midnight pick-me-up after a night out on the town.

Chicken Piccata with Artichokes

In this updated take on classic chicken piccata, savory artichoke hearts join the traditional lemon-caper sauce for added depth and texture. Tender chicken breasts are lightly floured and pan-fried until golden, then simmered in a bright, buttery sauce with white wine, lemon, and briny capers. The artichoke hearts add a delightful earthiness that complements the tangy sauce perfectly.

MAKES 6 SERVINGS

3 boneless, skinless chicken breasts, about 1½ pounds (680 g) total

½ cup (70 g) all-purpose flour

Kosher salt and freshly ground pepper

3 tablespoons (45 ml) olive oil

2 tablespoons (30 g) unsalted butter, at room temperature

2 garlic cloves, chopped

One 6-ounce (170 g) jar artichoke hearts, rinsed, drained, and quartered

1 cup (240 ml) dry white wine

½ cup (120 ml) low-sodium chicken broth

Juice of 1 lemon

2 tablespoons (16 g) capers, rinsed and drained

1 tablespoon (4 g) chopped fresh flat-leaf parsley

Butterfly the chicken breasts and cut them in half. Working with one chicken breast half at a time, place the chicken between two pieces of plastic wrap and, using a meat pounder or other heavy, flat object, gently pound to an even thickness of about ¼ inch (6 mm).

Pour the flour onto a large plate and season it well with salt and pepper. Dredge the chicken in the seasoned flour, shaking off the excess.

In a large fry pan over medium-high heat, warm 2 tablespoons (30 ml) of the olive oil until very hot but not smoking. Working in batches as needed to avoid crowding, add the chicken and cook, turning once, until golden brown on both sides and opaque throughout, about 4 minutes per side. Transfer to a plate and set aside.

Return the pan to medium-high heat; do not wipe the pan clean. Melt 1 tablespoon (15 g) of the butter with the remaining 1 tablespoon (15 ml) of olive oil. Add the garlic and artichoke hearts and sauté just until the garlic is soft, about 1 minute. Stir in the wine, scraping up any browned bits on the bottom of the pan. Bring to a simmer and cook until the liquid is reduced by half, about 3 minutes. Stir in the broth, lemon juice, and capers. Decrease the heat to medium, bring to a gentle simmer, and whisk in the remaining 1 tablespoon (15 g) of butter. Cook, stirring occasionally, until the sauce thickens slightly, about 5 minutes more. Stir in the parsley. Taste and adjust the seasoning.

Return the chicken to the pan and turn to coat each piece with the sauce. Cook just until the chicken is warmed through, about 2 minutes. Serve immediately.

Coq au Vin

A traditional dish from Burgundy, coq au vin is perfect for both cozy dinners and small parties. This version uses bone-in chicken thighs and drumsticks, which become exceptionally moist and tender after slow cooking in a Dutch oven.

MAKES 6 SERVINGS

6 ounces (170 g) thick-cut bacon, cut into ½-inch (13 mm) dice

2 pounds (910 g) bone-in chicken thighs

1½ pounds (680 g) chicken drumsticks

Kosher salt and freshly ground pepper

½ leek, cut lengthwise

1 pound (450 g) small button mushrooms

12 ounces (360 g) shallots, halved

3 garlic cloves, minced

2 tablespoons (30 g) tomato paste

2 tablespoons (16 g) all-purpose flour

1 bottle (750 ml) Pinot Noir

1¾ cups (420 ml) chicken broth

1 bay leaf

5 fresh flat-leaf parsley sprigs, plus 2 tablespoons (8 g) finely chopped parsley

3 fresh thyme sprigs

1 tablespoon (15 g) unsalted butter

12 ounces (360 g) carrots, peeled and cut into 2-inch (5 cm) pieces

Preheat the oven to 325°F (165°C).

In a large Dutch oven over medium heat, cook the bacon until crisp, about 8 minutes. Using a slotted spoon, transfer the bacon to a paper towel-lined plate, leaving the fat in the pot.

Season the chicken thighs and drumsticks generously with salt and pepper. Working in batches if necessary, add the chicken to the pot, skin side down, and cook until golden brown, about 5 minutes per side. Transfer the chicken to a plate and set aside.

Add the leek to the pot and cook, stirring occasionally, until softened, about 3 minutes. Add the mushrooms and cook until they begin to brown and release their liquid, about 5 minutes. Add the shallots and garlic and cook until fragrant, about 1 minute.

Stir in the tomato paste and cook for 1 minute. Sprinkle the flour over the vegetables and stir to coat, cooking for 1 to 2 minutes.

Pour in the Pinot Noir and chicken broth, stirring to scrape up any browned bits from the bottom of the pot. Add the bay leaf, parsley sprigs, and thyme sprigs. Bring to a simmer.

Return the chicken and any accumulated juices to the pot, along with the bacon and carrots. Nestle the chicken into the liquid, cover, and transfer to the oven. Braise until the chicken is very tender and falling off the bone, about 1½ to 2 hours.

Remove the pot from the oven and discard the bay leaf, parsley sprigs, and thyme sprigs. Stir in the butter. Taste and adjust the seasoning with salt and pepper.

Ladle into bowls, garnish with the chopped parsley, and serve immediately.

Simple Roast Chicken with Lemon

Roasting a whole chicken alongside fragrant lemons adds a fresh springtime twist to a comforting main dish. The citrus infuses the meat with bright flavor while creating aromatic pan juices perfect for drizzling over roasted vegetables or mashed potatoes.

MAKES 4 SERVINGS

One 4½-pound (2.3 kg) chicken
1 tablespoon (15 ml) olive oil
Zest of 1 lemon
Kosher salt and freshly ground pepper
4 garlic cloves
2 lemons, halved
1 large fresh thyme sprig
Fresh bay leaves, for garnish

Preheat the oven to 425°F (220°C).

Rinse the chicken inside and out and pat dry with paper towels. Combine the olive oil and and lemon zest. Rub the chicken all over–including the cavity–with the zest-infused oil, salt, and pepper. Put the garlic, 2 lemon halves, the bay leaf, and thyme sprig in the cavity. Tuck the wing tips behind the back. Tie the legs together with kitchen twine.

Put the chicken, breast side up, in a 4½-quart (4-L) deep baking dish. Insert a smart thermometer into the chicken breast according to the manufacturer's instructions. Place the remaining 4 lemon halves around the chicken. Cover the baking dish with the lid.

Transfer to the oven and roast the chicken until the thermometer registers 160°F (71°C), 1¼ to 1½ hours, removing the lid during the last 10 to 15 minutes of roasting.

Transfer the chicken to a carving board and let rest for 10 minutes. Pour the pan juices into a gravy boat. Carve the chicken and serve the juices alongside.

Pan-Roasted Beef Tenderloin with Rosemary and Garlic

Tender beef tenderloin gets the royal treatment with fresh rosemary and garlic and is then finished with a rich red wine pan sauce. The wine reduces down to concentrate its flavors, while butter and Dijon mustard create a glossy, restaurant-quality sauce that makes this roast unforgettable. Simple enough for a confident home cook, impressive enough for your most important occasions.

MAKES 6 SERVINGS

- One 2½- to 3-pound (1.1 to 1.4 kg) beef tenderloin roast
- 3 fresh rosemary sprigs
- 1 garlic clove, minced
- Salt and freshly ground pepper
- 1 tablespoon (15 ml) vegetable oil
- 4 shallots, minced
- 2 cups (480 ml) dry red wine
- 1 cup (240 g) softened unsalted butter, cut into ½-inch (13 mm) pieces

Preheat the oven to 400°F (200°C).

Let the roast stand at room temperature for 30 to 40 minutes.

Set the roast on a clean work surface and lay the rosemary sprigs lengthwise along the top. Using kitchen twine, tie the rosemary to the roast at 2-inch (5 cm) intervals. Rub the roast with the garlic and season with salt and pepper.

Preheat an oval skillet or large sauté pan over medium-high heat and warm the vegetable oil. Add the roast and brown, 3 to 4 minutes per side. Transfer the skillet to the oven and roast, turning the beef occasionally, until an instant-read thermometer inserted into the center of the meat registers 125°F (52°C) for very rare to rare, 15 to 20 minutes, or until done to your liking. Transfer the roast to a cutting board, cover loosely with aluminum foil, and let rest for 5 minutes.

Meanwhile, in a saucepan over medium-high heat, combine the shallots and wine and boil until reduced to ¼ cup (60 ml), 7 to 10 minutes. Add the butter a few pieces at a time, whisking constantly until blended before adding more. Strain the sauce through a fine-mesh sieve and season with salt. Keep warm over very low heat, being careful not to boil.

Slice the meat and arrange on a warmed platter. Pass the sauce alongside.

Fettuccine Alfredo

This Roman classic demands exceptional ingredients for authentic results. Choose unsalted European-style butter like Plugrà (found at gourmet stores) for its richer flavor and lower water content compared to standard brands. Select heavy cream that isn't ultra-pasteurized for superior taste, and request freshly cut Parmigiano-Reggiano from the wheel to ensure it hasn't dried out. In Italy, this indulgent dish appears in modest portions as a primi course—pair it with simple poached fish, baked seafood, or grilled meat for a perfectly balanced meal.

MAKES 6 SERVINGS

1½ cups (360 ml) heavy cream

5 tablespoons (75 g) unsalted butter

1 cup (100 g) grated Parmigiano-Reggiano cheese

Salt and freshly ground pepper

Freshly grated nutmeg

1 pound (450 g) homemade (page 95) or store-bought fresh fettuccine

In a large saucepan over high heat, bring the cream and butter to a boil. Decrease the heat to low and simmer for about 1 minute. Add 6 tablespoons (24 g) of the cheese and whisk until smooth, about 1 minute more. Remove from the heat and season with salt and pepper and a generous pinch of nutmeg. (Be judicious with the salt. Parmigiano-Reggiano is salty, so too much added salt will throw this creamy, sweet sauce out of balance.)

Meanwhile, bring a large pot of water to a boil over high heat. Generously salt the boiling water, add the pasta, and cook until al dente (tender but firm to the bite), 1 to 3 minutes, depending on the freshness of the pasta. Drain the pasta well.

Put the pasta in a warmed large, shallow bowl. Pour on the sauce, sprinkle with 6 tablespoons (24 g) of the cheese, and toss well. Serve immediately. Pass the remaining cheese at the table.

Homemade Fresh Pasta

This recipe uses an electric stand mixer to mix and knead the pasta dough, then relies on the mixer's specialized pasta attachments for rolling and cutting.

MAKES 1 POUND (450 G), 6 SERVINGS

2⅓ cups (325 g) all-purpose flour

1 cup (140 g) semolina flour

1 teaspoon salt

1 tablespoon (15 ml) olive oil

4 eggs

2 tablespoons (30 ml) water, plus more as needed

In the bowl of an electric mixer fitted with the flat beater, combine the all-purpose and semolina flours, salt, and olive oil. Beat on low speed just until combined, about 30 seconds.

In a small pitcher or other pourable container, whisk together the eggs and water. With the mixer on low speed, slowly drizzle in the egg mixture and beat until the flour has been absorbed into the egg mixture, about 2 minutes.

Stop the mixer and, using your hands, squeeze a small amount of dough into a ball. It should be moist enough to hold together but not sticky; if it is too dry, add more water, 1 teaspoon at a time.

Transfer the dough to a work surface and shape into two balls. Wrap separately with plastic wrap, then flatten each ball into a disk. Let stand at room temperature for at least 30 minutes or up to 2 hours.

Attach the pasta roller to the electric mixer according to the manufacturer's instructions.

Unwrap one dough disk and dust lightly with all-purpose flour. Using a rolling pin, roll out the dough into a rectangle about ½ inch (13 mm) thick and no wider than the pasta roller. Roll the dough through the rollers once at the widest setting, then lay the pasta on the work surface and fold it into thirds. Repeat the process two more times, rolling out the dough, rolling it through the rollers at the widest setting, and folding it into thirds each time.

Now thin the dough by rolling it through the rollers at the second-to-widest setting. Repeat, setting the rollers one notch narrower each time, until the desired thinness is reached. Transfer the dough to a baking sheet, cover loosely with plastic wrap, and roll out the other dough disk.

Attach a pasta cutter to the mixer according to the manufacturer's instructions and cut the pasta into the desired shape. If not cooking the pasta immediately, transfer it to a baking sheet and dust lightly with flour to prevent sticking. Cover tightly with plastic wrap and refrigerate for up to 24 hours.

Classic Macaroni and Cheese

Rich, creamy, and deeply satisfying, this classic baked macaroni and cheese features sharp white cheddar in a smooth, flavorful sauce with a crispy breadcrumb topping. A splash of dry sherry and a hint of nutmeg add subtle complexity that makes this version stand out from the rest.

MAKES 6 SERVINGS

4 cups (960 ml) milk

4 tablespoons (60 g) unsalted butter

½ cup (70 g) all-purpose flour

1 whole clove

1 bay leaf

1 white onion, peeled

2 cups (280 g) shredded sharp white cheddar cheese

Salt and freshly ground white pepper

Freshly grated nutmeg

2 teaspoons dry sherry

1 pound (450 g) dried macaroni

1 cup (115 g) breadcrumbs (see Note)

CHUCK'S TIP

Freshly grated nutmeg has so much more flavor than the already ground stuff. Buy whole nutmegs and grate them as needed with the fine rasps of a nutmeg grater, which includes a little compartment for holding the spice when not in use.

Position a rack in the upper third of the oven and preheat to 375°F (190°C). Butter a shallow 2-quart (1.8 L) baking dish.

In a saucepan over medium heat, warm the milk until bubbles begin to form around the edges of the pan. Keep warm.

In another medium saucepan over medium heat, melt the butter. When the foaming subsides, add the flour and cook, stirring constantly with a whisk or wooden spoon, until the flour and butter thicken into a paste and smell fragrant, about 1 minute. Do not let the roux brown. Slowly whisk in the milk until smooth and blended. Bring the sauce to a boil over medium heat, stirring constantly and scraping the bottom and sides of the pan to prevent lumping and scorching, then decrease the heat to low.

Using the clove, attach the bay leaf to the onion and add it to the sauce. Cook, stirring occasionally, until thickened, about 30 minutes. Remove and discard the onion, add 1 cup (140 g) of the cheese, and stir until blended. Season with salt, white pepper, and nutmeg, then add the sherry and stir until blended.

Meanwhile, bring a large pot three-fourths full of water to a boil over high heat. Add 1 tablespoon (15 g) of salt and the macaroni and cook according to the package instructions until al dente (tender but firm to the bite). Drain well.

Transfer the macaroni to the prepared baking dish. Spoon the sauce over the macaroni, scatter the remaining 1 cup (140 g) of cheese over the top, and sprinkle the breadcrumbs over the cheese. Bake, uncovered, until lightly browned and bubbling, 35 to 40 minutes. Serve immediately.

NOTE

For a crisp, golden crust, start with either stale or fresh bread slices, arranging them on a baking sheet and drying them in a 300°F (150°C) oven for 20 to 35 minutes until lightly toasted. Pulse the dried bread in a food processor to your preferred consistency, then season with salt and pepper.

Ruffoni Family Risotto with Porcini Mushrooms

While dried mushrooms offer convenient, year-round flavor in Italian cooking, autumn brings the incomparable luxury of fresh porcini mushrooms in creamy risotto. Their earthy, savory essence transforms this dish into something truly special. The Ruffoni family keeps quality rice, homemade stock, and their trusty copper risotto pan ready for when friends and family return from mushroom foraging to share the season's treasures together.

MAKES 4 SERVINGS

4 to 6 fresh or 1½ ounces (45 g) dried porcini mushrooms

Extra-virgin olive oil, as needed

1 shallot, finely chopped

1¼ cups (270 g) Carnaroli or arborio rice

½ cup (120 ml) white wine

6⅓ cups (1.5 L) beef stock, or as needed, warmed

Kosher salt

3 tablespoons (45 g) unsalted butter

3½ ounces (100 g) Parmigiano-Reggiano cheese, grated, plus more for serving

Chopped fresh flat-leaf parsley, for serving

Freshly ground pepper

CHUCK'S TIP

For a true risotto, you must use Italian arborio, Carnaroli, or Vialone Nano rice, a short-grained, starchy variety that gives the risotto its rich character and chewy texture.

If using dried mushrooms, soak them in lukewarm water for 1 hour to rehydrate them, then drain and discard the soaking water. Coarsely chop the mushrooms. If using fresh mushrooms, scrape the stems with a paring knife, removing any hard and woody parts, and brush off all the dirt. Leave the smaller stems whole or slice the larger ones lengthwise. Slice the mushroom tops.

In a chef's pan over low heat, warm a little olive oil. Add the shallot and cook, stirring occasionally, until translucent, 3 to 5 minutes; do not allow it to brown.

Add the rice and the rehydrated dried mushrooms, if using, and cook, stirring occasionally, until the rice smells warm and toasty and the edges become slightly translucent, about 3 minutes.

Increase the heat to medium and add the wine, stirring frequently until the alcohol evaporates. (The wine will leave behind a delicious flavor and balance the acidity in the rice.) Add a ladleful of stock and stir until the liquid is absorbed.

If using fresh mushrooms, add the stems. Add another ladleful of stock and cook, stirring constantly, until it is absorbed. Continue adding the stock a ladleful at a time, cooking and stirring until the liquid is absorbed, until the rice is almost tender, about 15 minutes. Taste and adjust the seasoning with salt. Add the sliced mushroom tops, reserving a few slices for garnish. Add another ladleful of stock, cooking and stirring until absorbed, then repeat with a final ladleful of stock.

Remove the pan from the heat and stir in the butter, Parmigiano-Reggiano, and parsley. Let the risotto rest for 1 to 2 minutes, then divide among wide, shallow bowls. Top with the reserved mushroom slices and a grinding of pepper. Serve immediately.

Beef Bourguignon with Boiled Potatoes and Parsley

In the traditional French version of this dish, mushrooms are lightly sautéed in butter and stirred in near the end. Here, we caramelize them first and add them to the braising base, which deepens the flavor. Choose a good-quality wine for this recipe—a simple rule applies: If you wouldn't drink it, don't cook with it.

MAKES 10 SERVINGS

3 tablespoons (45 ml) canola oil

One 4½-pound (2 kg) boneless chuck roast, cut into 1-inch (2.5 cm) cubes

Kosher salt and freshly ground pepper

1 pound (450 g) button mushrooms, quartered

8 ounces (225 g) slab bacon, cut into ¼-inch (6 mm) dice

1 large yellow onion, diced

2 teaspoons minced garlic

1½ tablespoons (23 ml) veal demi-glace

½ cup (70 g) all-purpose flour

1 bottle (750 ml) Pinot Noir

3 cups (720 ml) beef broth

1 pound (450 g) pearl onions, peeled

1 bouquet garni (2 bay leaves, 4 thyme sprigs, and 6 parsley sprigs, tied with kitchen twine)

3 tablespoons (12 g) chopped fresh flat-leaf parsley

1 recipe Boiled Potatoes with Parsley (page 101), for serving

Preheat the oven to 350°F (180°C).

In a 6¾-quart (6 L) Dutch oven over medium-high heat, warm 2 tablespoons (30 ml) of the oil until just smoking. Season the beef with salt and pepper. Working in batches, brown the beef on all sides, 10 to 12 minutes per batch. Transfer to a large bowl.

Add the remaining 1 tablespoon (15 ml) of oil and the mushrooms to the pot and cook, stirring occasionally, until well browned, 6 to 8 minutes, adding 1 to 2 tablespoons (15 to 30 ml) of water if the bottom of the pot becomes too dark. Transfer the mushrooms to the bowl with the beef.

Decrease the heat to medium and add the bacon to the pot. Cook, stirring occasionally, until the bacon is browned and crisp, 6 to 8 minutes. Transfer the bacon to the bowl with the beef and mushrooms.

Discard all but ¼ cup (60 ml) of the fat from the pot. Add the yellow onion and cook, stirring occasionally, until softened, 6 to 8 minutes. Add the garlic, demi-glace, and flour and cook, stirring constantly, until fragrant, about 1 minute. Slowly whisk in the wine and cook, stirring occasionally, for 20 minutes.

Return the beef, mushrooms, and bacon to the pot. Add the broth, pearl onions, and bouquet garni. Season with salt and pepper and bring to a simmer. Cover the pot with aluminum foil and then with the lid. Transfer to the oven and cook until the meat is fork-tender, 2½ to 3 hours.

Skim the excess fat off the sauce and remove and discard the bouquet garni. Adjust the seasonings with salt and pepper. Sprinkle with the parsley. Serve the stew immediately over boiled potatoes.

Boiled Potatoes and Parsley

Boiled potatoes are the perfect accompaniment to hearty stews like Beef Bourguignon. Crisp on the outside and tender within, they soak up rich sauces beautifully.

MAKES 8 SERVINGS

3 pounds (1.4 kg) Yukon gold potatoes, each about 2 inches (5 cm) in diameter, peeled

Kosher salt

4 tablespoons (60 g) unsalted butter, melted

3 tablespoons (12 g) chopped fresh flat-leaf parsley

Put the potatoes in a large pot and add water to cover the potatoes by 2 inches (5 cm). Season the water with salt and bring to a boil over medium-high heat. Decrease the heat to medium-low and simmer until the potatoes are tender when pierced, 10 to 12 minutes.

Drain the potatoes well and transfer to a serving bowl. Add the butter and parsley and toss to coat. Serve immediately.

Potato Leek Gratin

Prepared with cream and two kinds of cheeses, this rich gratin makes a decadent side dish for your Thanksgiving feast or your favorite roast meats. The golden, bubbling top and creamy interior create the perfect balance of textures that will have guests coming back for seconds.

MAKES 8 SERVINGS

- 5 tablespoons (75 g) unsalted butter
- 4 pounds (1.8 kg) leeks, white and light green portions, rinsed well, cut into ¼-inch (6 mm) rings
- 1 to 2 teaspoons (15 g) kosher salt
- 1 teaspoon minced fresh thyme
- ¾ teaspoon freshly ground pepper, plus more as needed
- ¼ teaspoon freshly grated nutmeg
- 1 cup (240 ml) heavy cream
- 1½ cups (210 g) grated Gruyère cheese
- ¾ cup (75 g) grated Parmesan cheese
- 3 pounds (1.4 kg) russet potatoes, peeled and cut into ¼-inch (6 mm) slices
- 3 tablespoons (6 g) minced fresh chives

In a large fry pan over medium heat, melt 4 tablespoons (60 g) of the butter. Add the leeks and salt, stirring to coat the leeks with the butter. Cover and cook, stirring occasionally, until the leeks are tender, about 20 minutes. Add the thyme, pepper, nutmeg, and cream and simmer, uncovered, stirring occasionally, until thickened, about 15 minutes. Transfer to a bowl and let cool.

Preheat the oven to 400°F (200°C). Grease a 9-inch (23 cm) square baking dish or large gratin dish with the remaining 1 tablespoon (15 g) of butter.

In a bowl, combine the Gruyère and Parmesan cheeses. Layer one-third of the potatoes in the baking dish and spread one-third of the leek mixture on top. Sprinkle with one-third of the cheeses, then 1 tablespoon (2 g) of the chives. Repeat the layering two more times. Top with several grindings of pepper.

Cover the dish with aluminum foil, transfer to the oven, and bake for 45 minutes. Remove the foil and continue baking until the potatoes are tender and the crust is golden brown, about 30 minutes more. Let the gratin stand for 15 minutes before serving.

The Bounty of the Garden

Vegetarian, Plant-Based, Salads, and Sides

Vegetables have stepped into the spotlight in today's kitchens, no longer relegated to supporting roles but celebrated as the stars they've always deserved to be. These recipes celebrate vegetables in all their glory—from the elegant simplicity of Pan-Roasted Asparagus with Garlic and Lemon Zest (page 118) that lets the vegetable's natural sweetness shine to the creative artistry of our Modern Niçoise Salad (page 116) that reimagines a classic without sacrificing any of its sophisticated appeal. Each dish proves that plant-based cooking can be every bit as satisfying and luxurious as any meal centered around meat or fish.

Blistered Tomato Caprese with Burrata

This Italian classic traditionally pairs tomatoes, fresh mozzarella, and basil in elegant simplicity. Our playful variation quickly sautés cherry and Campari tomatoes in a hot pan until they burst and soften, intensifying their natural flavors. We crown the salad with burrata—a luxurious cow's milk cheese similar to mozzarella but with an irresistibly creamy interior. Serve with crusty bread to capture every drop of the flavorful juices. For larger tomatoes, cut them into wedges before cooking to ensure even-size pieces throughout.

MAKES 6 SERVINGS

½ cup (120 ml) extra-virgin olive oil, plus more for drizzling

2 pounds (1 kg) cherry and Campari tomatoes

Kosher salt

8 ounces (240 g) burrata, at room temperature

Flaky sea salt and freshly ground pepper

Fresh tarragon, basil, or oregano leaves and/or sprigs, for garnish

In a frying pan over medium-high heat, warm the olive oil until small bubbles form around the edges. Add half of the tomatoes and cook, tossing occasionally, until the skins have just burst and the tomatoes are softened, about 3 minutes. Season with a sprinkling of kosher salt. Transfer to a serving platter or bowl and cover with aluminum foil. Repeat with the remaining tomatoes and transfer to the platter.

Top the tomatoes with the burrata, drizzle with olive oil, and sprinkle with flaky sea salt and pepper. Scatter the tarragon over the salad and serve immediately.

Farmers' Market Salad with Whipped Ricotta

This uncomplicated salad combines Little Gem lettuce, fennel, cherry tomatoes, and watermelon radishes with a bright lemony dressing, all served over a cloud of whipped ricotta for creamy contrast. Fresh and invigorating, it captures the essence of the season in every bite.

MAKES 4 SERVINGS

WHIPPED RICOTTA

1 cup (240 g) whole-milk ricotta cheese

1 tablespoon (15 ml) extra-virgin olive oil

Zest of ½ Meyer lemon

1 garlic clove

¼ teaspoon kosher salt

MEYER LEMON DRESSING

Juice of 1 Meyer lemon

¼ cup (60 ml) extra-virgin olive oil

1 tablespoon (15 g) wildflower honey

Pinch of kosher salt

SALAD

6 ounces (180 g) Little Gem lettuce, leaves separated

½ fennel bulb, halved lengthwise and thinly sliced on a mandoline, fennel flowers or fronds reserved for garnish

1 handful golden cherry tomatoes, halved

1 watermelon radish, thinly sliced on a mandoline

Kosher salt and freshly ground pepper

1 Hass avocado, pitted, peeled, and cut into ½-inch (13 mm) slices

Small handful dill flowers, for garnish

To make the whipped ricotta: In a food processor, combine the ricotta, olive oil, lemon zest, garlic, and salt. Process until smooth and combined, about 30 seconds.

To make the Meyer lemon dressing: In a small bowl, whisk together the lemon juice, olive oil, honey, and salt until emulsified. Taste and adjust the seasoning with salt.

Using a spoon, place large dollops of the whipped ricotta on a serving platter. Smear the ricotta artfully with the spoon to make swirly divots in the cheese; this will spread the ricotta out evenly and create indentations to capture the dressing. Drizzle about one-third of the dressing over the ricotta.

To make the salad: In a medium bowl, combine the lettuce, sliced fennel, tomatoes, and radish. Add a few pinches of salt and a few grindings of pepper and toss gently until combined. Drizzle on as much of the remaining dressing as you like; you can start with a little, then taste and add more as desired.

Transfer the salad in a pile on top of the ricotta, allowing a little bit of the cheese to remain visible on the sides of the platter. Arrange the avocado slices on the salad. Garnish with the fennel flowers or fronds and dill flowers. Add a few grindings of pepper and serve immediately.

Roasted Carrots with Pistachios and Hot Honey

Ideal for autumn entertaining, this vibrant side dish proves that simple ingredients can create spectacular flavors. Rainbow carrots roast in a hot oven until their natural sweetness intensifies, then get drizzled with spicy hot honey for a delicious kick. Crushed pistachios provide the perfect crunchy finishing touch. A small food processor quickly transforms whole pistachios into the ideal texture for sprinkling.

MAKES 12 SERVINGS

1½ pounds (680 g) rainbow carrots, peeled and cut lengthwise into similar sizes, ideally ½ inch (13 mm) thick (some nice-looking stems left intact)

⅓ cup (80 ml) extra-virgin olive oil

Kosher salt and freshly ground pepper

⅓ cup (80 g) hot honey, store-bought

3 tablespoons (30 g) pulverized roasted salted pistachios

Preheat the oven to 425°F (220°C).

In a large bowl, toss the carrots with the olive oil and a generous pinch of salt and pepper. Arrange the carrots in a single layer on a rimmed baking sheet.

Roast for 15 minutes, then toss the carrots. Continue roasting until they are charred and caramelized on the outside and tender on the inside, about 15 minutes more.

Meanwhile, in a small saucepan over medium-high heat, bring the hot honey to a vigorous simmer to thin it out.

Remove the baking sheet from the oven, pour half of the simmering hot honey over the carrots, and roast until nicely caramelized, about 5 minutes more.

Transfer the carrots to a serving platter, drizzle with the remaining hot honey, and dust with the pistachios. Serve immediately.

Crispy Cauliflower Steaks with Lemon and Parmesan

Cauliflower has stepped out from the shadows to join kale and other trendy brassicas in the culinary spotlight. Sliced into thick "steaks," coated with flavorful seasonings, and lightly fried before oven-roasting, it develops an irresistibly crispy exterior. This substantial dish makes an impressive side or a satisfying vegetarian main course.

MAKES 12 SERVINGS

Kosher salt

1 large head cauliflower, about 2 pounds (1 kg), cut crosswise into 4 slices

2 eggs

1 tablespoon (15 g) Dijon mustard

1¼ cups (125 g) panko

¾ cup (75 g) grated Parmesan cheese, plus more for serving

2 teaspoons onion powder

2 teaspoons garlic powder

½ teaspoon smoked paprika

1 teaspoon freshly ground pepper

½ teaspoon grated lemon zest

Olive oil, for frying

1 lemon, thinly sliced

Mixed fresh herb leaves, such as flat-leaf parsley, basil, and thyme, for serving

Preheat the oven to 375°F (190°C).

Bring a large pot of salted water to a boil over high heat. Add the cauliflower slices and cook until tender but not mushy, 5 to 7 minutes. Transfer to a paper towel–lined plate and dry well.

In a shallow bowl, whisk together the eggs and mustard. In another shallow bowl, whisk together the panko, Parmesan, onion powder, garlic powder, paprika, 1 teaspoon salt, 1 teaspoon pepper, and the lemon zest.

Place a wire rack on a baking sheet. In a large frying pan over medium-high heat, pour in the olive oil to a depth of ½ inch (13 mm) and heat until just beginning to smoke. Working in batches, dip the cauliflower slices in the egg mixture, allowing any excess to drip off. Then coat with the panko mixture, pressing so that it adheres. Fry the cauliflower, turning once, until golden brown and crisp, about 3 minutes per side. Transfer the cauliflower to the rack-lined baking sheet and scatter the lemon slices around the cauliflower. Roast in the oven until the cauliflower is heated through and very crisp, about 5 minutes.

Transfer the cauliflower steaks and lemon slices to a serving platter. Sprinkle with more Parmesan, garnish with herb leaves, and serve.

Greek Salad with Feta and Kalamata Olives

Each Mediterranean olive oil–producing region crafts distinctive styles—Greek oils offer rich mellowness, Tuscan varieties deliver peppery intensity, and Sicilian oils are bold and earthy, while French southern coast oils taste buttery and smooth. Match oil character to your dish: delicate oils enhance light salads, vegetables, and fish, while robust varieties complement hearty vegetables, anchovies, garlic, dark greens, and red meats for optimal flavor harmony.

MAKES 8 SERVINGS

2 red bell peppers

1 green bell pepper

2 cups (150 g) cherry tomatoes

2 cucumbers

2 red onions

8 ounces (240 g) feta cheese

¾ (75 g) cup Kalamata olives

6 anchovy fillets (optional)

2 tablespoons (16 g) capers, rinsed

¼ cup (60 ml) red wine vinegar

1 garlic clove, minced

2 tablespoons (6 g) minced fresh dill

1 teaspoon dried oregano

½ teaspoon salt

½ teaspoon freshly ground pepper

⅓ cup (80 ml) fruity extra-virgin olive oil

Seed the bell peppers and cut them into 1-inch (2.5 cm) chunks. Stem the cherry tomatoes and halve one-half of them, leaving the others whole. Peel and thickly slice the cucumbers and thinly slice the red onions. Cut the feta cheese into 1-inch (2.5 cm) cubes.

In a large bowl, combine the bell peppers, tomatoes, cucumbers, onions, feta cheese, olives, anchovies (if desired), and capers and toss together.

In a small bowl, whisk together the vinegar, garlic, dill, oregano, salt, and pepper. While whisking, slowly drizzle in the olive oil to make a thick dressing. Pour the dressing over the salad, toss, and serve immediately.

Chuck's Waldorf Salad

Oscar Tschirky, maître d' of New York City's original Waldorf-Astoria Hotel, invented Waldorf salad using equal parts chopped apples and celery bound with mayonnaise. The addition of walnuts boosted the salad's appeal, and subsequent generations have adapted the recipe with contemporary ingredients to suit evolving tastes. Throughout the eastern United States, this classic has earned its place on Thanksgiving tables, providing a refreshing counterpoint to the holiday's rich feast.

MAKES 12 SERVINGS

¾ cup (35 g) walnut or pecan halves

4 crisp apples, such as Pippin, McIntosh, or Rome Beauty

Juice of 1 lemon

1 cup (120 g) finely diced celery

½ cup (70 g) diced red bell pepper

3 green onions, including some of the tender green portions, finely chopped

¾ cup (180 g) sour cream

1 tablespoon (15 g) Dijon mustard

1½ tablespoons (23 g) honey

1 teaspoon minced fresh mint

Salt and freshly ground pepper

1 or 2 heads Bibb lettuce

1 head radicchio

Preheat the oven to 200°F (95°C). Spread the nuts on a baking sheet and bake until lightly toasted, 6 to 7 minutes. Set aside to cool.

Peel, core, and quarter the apples, then cut into thin slices. In a bowl, toss the apples with the lemon juice. Add the celery, bell pepper, green onions, and nuts and stir to combine.

In another bowl, combine the sour cream, mustard, honey, and mint. Whisk until well blended, and then season with salt and pepper.

Separate the lettuce and radicchio leaves and use only the crisp inner leaves; reserve the larger outer leaves for another use. Arrange the lettuce and radicchio leaves around the rim of a serving platter. Mound the apple and vegetable mixture in the center. Drizzle the dressing over the top rather than mixing it in, then garnish with the whole nuts. Spoon the salad onto the center of the platter.

Modern Niçoise Salad

This stunning composed salad from Provence classically showcases tuna and anchovies alongside vibrant vegetables. Our contemporary take eliminates the seafood and introduces crisp fennel slices for added texture and flavor.

MAKES 4 SERVINGS

DIJON VINAIGRETTE

1 shallot, diced

¼ cup (60 ml) white balsamic vinegar or white wine vinegar

2 teaspoons Dijon mustard

Kosher salt and freshly ground pepper

½ cup (120 ml) extra-virgin olive oil

2 teaspoons mayonnaise

SALAD

1 pound (450 g) baby yellow potatoes, halved

3 tablespoons (45 ml) extra-virgin olive oil, plus more as needed

Kosher salt and freshly ground pepper

1 fennel bulb, trimmed, cored, and thinly sliced on a mandoline, fronds reserved for garnish

1 pint (360 g) cherry tomatoes, halved

2 heads Belgian endive

2 cups (60 g) mixed greens

8 ounces (240 g) haricots verts, blanched

½ cup (60 g) Castelvetrano olives

2 hard-boiled eggs (see page 56), peeled and halved

1 tablespoon (8 g) capers

Preheat the oven to 400°F (200°C).

To make the Dijon vinaigrette: In a small bowl, combine the shallot and vinegar and let stand for 5 minutes. Whisk in the mustard and season with salt and pepper. Slowly drizzle in the olive oil, whisking constantly until incorporated, then whisk in the mayonnaise.

To make the salad: In a medium bowl, stir together the potatoes and olive oil and season with salt and pepper. Transfer to a baking sheet and roast until the potatoes are tender and the cut sides are golden brown and crisp, 20 to 25 minutes. Let cool.

In a small bowl, stir together the fennel and 2 tablespoons (30 ml) of the vinaigrette. In a medium bowl, stir together the tomatoes and 2 tablespoons (30 ml) of the vinaigrette. Using separate bowls for each, repeat with the endive, mixed greens, and haricots verts.

To assemble the salad, arrange the potatoes, fennel, tomatoes, endive, mixed greens, haricots verts, olives, and hard-boiled eggs in separate piles on a large serving platter. Drizzle with the remaining vinaigrette and season with salt and pepper. Garnish with the capers and fennel fronds and serve.

CHUCK'S TIP

A signature dish from Nice, the traditional version was made with only raw vegetables. If you can find them, the slender, true French haricots verts are the best variety to use.

Pan-Roasted Asparagus with Garlic and Lemon Zest

Fresh asparagus makes a perfect tribute to spring's arrival, reaching peak season from March through May. To trim the spears properly, simply bend each thick end until it naturally snaps at the tender point. For a more polished look, slice a thin piece from the base of each trimmed spear.

MAKES 4 SERVINGS

2 tablespoons (30 g) unsalted butter

3 tablespoons (45 ml) olive oil

1 pound (450 g) asparagus, tough ends trimmed

Kosher salt and freshly ground pepper

3 garlic cloves

1 tablespoon (6 g) grated lemon zest

½ cup (55 g) panko (Japanese breadcrumbs)

Preheat the broiler or preheat the oven to 500°F (260°C).

In a large ovenproof frying pan over medium-high heat, melt the butter with 1 tablespoon (15 ml) of the olive oil. Arrange the asparagus in a single layer in the pan and sprinkle with salt and pepper to taste. Sauté the asparagus, turning it frequently, until the asparagus is crisp-tender, 5 to 8 minutes, depending on the thickness of the spears.

While the asparagus is sautéing, in a mini food processor, combine the garlic, lemon zest, panko, and remaining 2 tablespoons (30 ml) of olive oil. Pulse until the garlic is finely chopped and the ingredients are thoroughly combined.

When the asparagus is crisp-tender, sprinkle the panko mixture over the top. Transfer the pan to the oven and broil or roast until the topping is golden brown, 1 to 2 minutes.

Transfer the asparagus to a serving dish, if desired, or serve directly from the pan. Serve immediately.

Braised Artichokes with Horseradish Aioli

Smooth aioli enhanced with gently spicy horseradish provides an ideal partner for earthy artichokes, those herald-of-spring vegetables that signal the season's arrival at farmers' markets. Prepare the aioli up to 3 days ahead and refrigerate, covered, until ready to serve.

MAKES 4 SERVINGS

AIOLI

1 egg yolk

1 garlic clove

Kosher salt and freshly ground pepper

½ cup (120 ml) vegetable oil

¼ teaspoon cayenne pepper, plus more to taste

2 tablespoons (30 g) prepared horseradish, plus more to taste

ARTICHOKES

½ lemon

4 large artichokes

4 tablespoons (60 g) unsalted butter

6 garlic cloves

3 fresh thyme sprigs

1 cup (240 ml) white wine

3 cups (720 ml) chicken stock

Kosher salt and freshly ground pepper

To make the aioli: In a small food processor, combine the egg yolk, garlic, and a pinch each of salt and pepper. Pulse several times until the garlic is finely chopped and the ingredients are combined. With the machine running, slowly add a few drops of the oil, then follow with a slow and steady stream of oil until the mixture is thoroughly combined. Transfer to a bowl and stir in the cayenne and horseradish, adding more to taste if desired. Season with salt and pepper. Cover and refrigerate until ready to use.

To make the artichokes: Fill a bowl with water and squeeze the juice from the lemon half into it. Working with one artichoke at a time, snap off the dark green leaves until you reach the tender yellow inner leaves. Using a small, sharp knife, pare away any tough green patches from the bottom of the artichoke, then cut off the top 2 inches (5 cm) of the artichoke. Cut the artichoke in half lengthwise, then scoop out the fuzzy choke. Drop the artichoke halves into the lemon water as you finish trimming them to prevent them from discoloring.

In a large sauté pan over medium-high heat, melt the butter. Add the artichokes, garlic, and thyme and cook, stirring occasionally, until the artichokes are golden brown all over, about 4 minutes. Add the wine and chicken stock and a pinch each of salt and pepper. Bring to a boil, then decrease the heat to low, cover, and simmer until the artichokes are very tender, 25 to 30 minutes.

Remove the artichokes from the liquid and cut each piece in half lengthwise. Sprinkle the aioli lightly with cayenne, if desired, and serve the artichokes with the aioli alongside.

Crispy Stacked Potatoes with Herbs

Ideal for holiday gatherings, this crowd-pleasing side is both elegant and practical. A mandoline quickly cuts the potatoes into thin, even slices, while clarified butter—with its higher smoke point than regular butter—prevents scorching in the hot oven.

MAKES 12 SERVINGS

10 large russet potatoes, peeled

2 tablespoons (8 g) minced fresh herbs, such as thyme, sage, tarragon, and rosemary

1½ to 2 teaspoons kosher salt, plus more to taste

Freshly ground pepper

¼ cup (60 ml) clarified butter

Flaky sea salt

Preheat the oven to 400°F (200°C).

Working with one potato at a time, using a mandoline, thinly slice the potatoes into slices about ⅛ inch (3 mm) thick, gathering the slices together as you go to retain the potato's shape as much as possible.

Carefully arrange the potato slices vertically in a 12-inch (30 cm) cast-iron skillet, starting at the edges of the of the pan and moving in toward the center. Then, using your hands, press down lightly on the potatoes to tilt them slightly, as if they were dominoes that are beginning to topple over.

Scatter the herbs over the potatoes, tucking some of them between the slices, then sprinkle the kosher salt evenly on top and season generously with pepper. Using a spoon, arrange dollops of the clarified butter evenly over the surface of the potatoes.

Bake, uncovered, until the potatoes are browned on the edges and tender in the middle when tested with a skewer, about 1 hour. Sprinkle lightly with flaky sea salt and serve immediately.

CHUCK'S TIP

A mandoline is, for lack of a better description, a manually operated food processor. It takes its name from the strumming action the cook uses as he or she moves a vegetable up and down the mandoline's stainless-steel, wooden, or plastic frame, past a precisely set, adjustable stainless-steel cutting blade that produces slices of uniform thickness.

Broccolini and Garlic with Calabrian Chile Vinaigrette

This versatile side tastes just as delicious warm as it does at room temperature, making it ideal for effortless summer entertaining. If you don't have a large steamer basket, simply cook the broccolini in two batches. To get ahead, prepare the vinaigrette and steam the broccolini up to a day in advance, storing them separately. Just before serving, toss everything together and finish as directed.

MAKES 4 SERVINGS

VINAIGRETTE

1 tablespoon (15 g) Calabrian chiles in oil, chopped

Juice of ½ small lemon

1 tablespoon (15 g) wildflower honey

2 tablespoons (30 ml) extra-virgin olive oil

Kosher salt

BROCCOLINI

10 garlic cloves, peeled and halved lengthwise

1 pound (450 g) broccolini, trimmed

Kosher salt

To make the vinaigrette: In a bowl, combine the Calabrian chiles, lemon juice, honey, and olive oil. Whisk until the vinaigrette is emulsified. Season with salt and set aside.

To make the broccolini: Fill a large, wide pot with 1 inch (2.5 cm) of water. Place a large steamer basket in the pot and cover the pot with a lid. Bring the water to a boil over high heat. Once the water comes to a boil, turn the heat to medium-low.

Remove the lid and add the garlic cloves to the steamer basket. Cover and steam the garlic for 6 minutes. Carefully remove the lid and, using tongs, quickly place the broccolini in the steamer basket. Cover and steam until the broccolini is a vibrant green and both the broccolini and the garlic are tender, about 4 minutes.

Transfer the broccolini and garlic to a large bowl and season lightly with salt. Add the vinaigrette and, using tongs, gently toss until the broccolini and garlic are evenly coated.

To serve the dish at room temperature: Transfer the broccolini and garlic to a serving platter and top with any remaining vinaigrette from the mixing bowl. Let stand at room temperature for 15 to 20 minutes before serving.

To serve the dish hot: Position a rack in the top third of the oven and preheat the broiler to high. Transfer the broccolini mixture to a baking sheet. Broil until the broccolini is slightly charred, about 4 minutes. Transfer to a serving platter and top with any remaining vinaigrette from the baking sheet.

Pickled Jalapeños and Carrots

Often known as escabeche, this zesty condiment pairs beautifully with tacos or any favorite Tex-Mex dish—just set it out and let everyone help themselves. The beauty of this recipe is that the flavor deepens as it sits, so it's best made ahead of time.

MAKES ABOUT 3 CUPS (360 G)

1½ cups (360 ml) distilled white vinegar

¼ cup (50 g) sugar

½ teaspoon kosher salt

1 bay leaf

5 peppercorns

3 jalapeño chiles, cut into ⅛-inch (3 mm) slices

1 large carrot, peeled and cut on the diagonal into ¼-inch (6 mm) slices

½ red onion, sliced

In a saucepan over medium heat, combine the vinegar, sugar, salt, bay leaf, and peppercorns and cook, stirring once or twice, until the sugar and salt dissolve, about 2 minutes.

Add the jalapeños, carrot, and onion and decrease the heat to low. Cook, stirring occasionally, until the vegetables are soft, about 1½ hours. Using a slotted spoon, transfer the pickles to a serving bowl and let cool. Serve immediately or store in an airtight container in the refrigerator, with enough pickling liquid to cover, for up to 2 weeks.

The Flavors of the World

Global Flavors and Traditions

Ve invite you on a culinary journey across continents, celebrating the ich diversity of global cooking. From the bright, herb-filled freshness of 'ietnamese Fresh Spring Rolls (page 149) to the warming spices of Acorn quash Dal with Cashew-Cilantro Rice (page 145), each recipe offers a glimpse nto a unique culinary tradition. Savor the umami comfort of Miso Soup with lack Cod and Green Onions (page 150), the bold heat of Korean-Style Grilled hort Ribs with Gochujang Peanut Sauce (page 143), and the elegant simplicity f Sicilian Sea Bass in Tomatoes with Fried Capers (page 134).

Thai Green Chicken Curry with Asparagus

Thai green curry paste delivers bold, concentrated flavor and heat, but when mellowed with rich, creamy coconut milk, it transforms into a fragrant simmer sauce for tender spring chicken, fresh asparagus, and aromatic Thai basil. Serve it with steamed jasmine rice to soak up every last drop of the luscious sauce.

MAKES 6 SERVINGS

Kosher salt

1½ pounds (680 g) asparagus, trimmed and cut into 2-inch (5 cm) pieces

4 boneless, skinless chicken breast halves

2 tablespoons (30 ml) peanut or grapeseed oil

1 yellow onion, cut into 8 wedges

1 small red bell pepper, seeded and cut into matchsticks

½-inch (13 mm) piece fresh ginger, peeled and minced

2 garlic cloves, minced

One 13½-ounce (405 g) can unsweetened coconut milk (unshaken)

3 tablespoons (45 g) Thai green curry paste

1 cup (240 ml) chicken broth

2 tablespoons (30 ml) Asian fish sauce

½ cup (20 g) small Thai basil leaves

1 lime, cut into wedges

Bring a saucepan of salted water to a boil over high heat. Add the asparagus and cook just until crisp-tender, about 2 minutes. Drain and refresh with cold water, then drain again. Cut the chicken across the grain on a slight diagonal into slices about ½ inch (13 mm) thick. Season with salt.

In a large frying pan over medium-high heat, warm the oil. Add the onion and bell pepper and cook, stirring frequently, until beginning to soften, about 3 minutes. Stir in the ginger and garlic and cook, stirring frequently, until fragrant, about 30 seconds. Transfer to a plate.

Open the can of coconut milk (do not shake it) and scoop out 3 tablespoons (45 g) of the thick cream on the top. Return the pan to medium-high heat. Add the coconut cream and curry paste and stir well. Whisk in the remaining coconut milk, broth, and fish sauce.

Return the onion mixture to the pan, stir in the chicken, and bring to a boil. Decrease the heat to medium-low and simmer, stirring occasionally, until the sauce has reduced slightly and the vegetables are crisp-tender, about 5 minutes. Stir in the asparagus and cook until the chicken is opaque throughout, about 3 minutes. Adjust the seasoning and serve immediately, garnished with the basil and lime wedges.

Spanish Paella with Chorizo and Seafood

Packed with three types of seafood and spicy chorizo, this Spanish paella is guaranteed to satisfy a hungry crowd. The recipe features Bomba rice—a short-grain Spanish variety prized for its ability to soak up nearly three times its volume in liquid while staying firm and flavorful—but any traditional paella rice will work beautifully.

MAKES 4 TO 6 SERVINGS

2 tablespoons (30 ml) olive oil

1 pound (450 g) Spanish chorizo or other spicy smoked sausages, cut into slices ½ inch (13 mm) thick

1 yellow onion, chopped

1 red bell pepper, seeded and chopped

3 garlic cloves, minced

Kosher salt and freshly ground pepper

2 cups (440 g) Bomba rice or other Spanish paella rice

½ teaspoon saffron threads

4 cups (960 ml) chicken broth

1 pound (450 g) jumbo shrimp

1 pound (450 g) small clams, such as littleneck or Manila, scrubbed

1 pound (450 g) mussels, scrubbed and debearded

1 cup (155 g) frozen peas

In a large paella pan or a large sauté pan over medium-high heat, warm the olive oil. Add the sausage and cook, turning occasionally, until browned on both sides, about 3 minutes. Add the onion, bell pepper, and garlic and cook, stirring occasionally, until softened, 3 to 4 minutes. Season with salt and pepper.

Add the rice, crumble in the saffron, and cook, stirring, until the grains are well coated, about 2 minutes. Pour in the broth and stir in 1½ teaspoons of salt. Bring to a boil, then decrease the heat to low, cover, and cook until the rice has absorbed nearly all of the liquid, about 20 minutes.

While the rice is cooking, using a sharp paring knife or kitchen shears, cut along each shrimp's shell above the vein line and then remove the vein. Leave the shell and tail intact.

When the rice has absorbed nearly all of the liquid, press the clams and mussels, hinge sides down, into the rice, discarding any that do not close to the touch. Spread the shrimp over the rice and top with the peas. Cover and cook until the shrimp are opaque and the clams have opened, about 5 minutes. Discard any unopened clams and mussels and serve immediately.

CHUCK'S TIP

You can make paella fairly easily and without throwing in everything but the kitchen sink. The best paella I ever ate was in a little place north of Barcelona—it consisted of rice, pungent seasonings, and a sauce made from sun-ripened tomatoes, cooked in a layer no more than 1 inch (2.5 cm) thick in a huge paella pan.

Greek Moussaka

Moussaka is a perfect choice for feeding a crowd, and much of the work can be done ahead of time. Make the meat sauce and béchamel the night before, then gently rewarm them before assembling. Once baked, the dish not only holds beautifully but often tastes even better the next day.

MAKES 6 SERVINGS

2½ pounds (1.3 kg) globe eggplant (2 medium), cut crosswise into slices ¼ inch (6 mm) thick

6 tablespoons (90 ml) plus 1 teaspoon olive oil, plus more for brushing

Kosher salt and freshly ground pepper

3 tablespoons (45 g) unsalted butter

3 tablespoons (24 g) all-purpose flour

1 bay leaf

¼ teaspoon freshly grated nutmeg

2 cups (480 ml) milk

1 egg, lightly beaten

5 tablespoons (30 g) grated Parmigiano-Reggiano cheese

Position racks in the upper, middle, and lower positions of the oven. Preheat the oven to 450°F (230°C). Line three baking sheets with parchment paper.

Arrange the eggplant slices in a single layer on the prepared baking sheets. Brush the slices on both sides with 5 tablespoons (75 ml) of the olive oil and season with salt and pepper. Roast until the eggplant is tender and lightly browned, about 20 minutes, rotating the baking sheets among the racks about every 7 minutes.

Meanwhile, in a saucepan over medium heat, melt the butter. Add the flour, bay leaf, and nutmeg and cook, stirring constantly, for 1 minute. Slowly whisk in the milk and cook, stirring constantly, until thickened, about 5 minutes. Season with salt and pepper. Let the sauce cool for 15 minutes, then remove and discard the bay leaf. Whisk in the egg and 2 tablespoons (12 g) of the cheese. Set the béchamel sauce aside.

- 1 yellow onion, diced
- 1½ pounds (680 g) ground lamb
- 1½ teaspoons minced garlic
- 1 tablespoon (15 g) tomato paste
- 1 teaspoon ground cinnamon
- ¼ teaspoon ground allspice
- ¼ teaspoon cayenne pepper
- 1½ teaspoons sugar
- One 14½-ounce (435 g) can diced tomatoes, drained
- 3 tablespoons (12 g) chopped fresh flat-leaf parsley

In a 3½-quart (3 L) Dutch oven over medium heat, warm 1 tablespoon (15 ml) of the olive oil. Add the onion and cook, stirring occasionally, until tender, 7 to 8 minutes. Transfer to a bowl. Increase the heat to medium-high and warm the remaining 1 teaspoon of olive oil. Add the ground lamb and cook, stirring occasionally, until browned, about 8 minutes. Drain off the excess fat. Add the garlic, tomato paste, cinnamon, allspice, cayenne, and sugar and cook, stirring constantly, for 1 minute. Add the tomatoes, season with salt and pepper, and cook for 3 to 4 minutes more. Stir in 2 tablespoons (8 g) of the parsley. Transfer the meat sauce to the bowl with the onion.

Decrease the oven temperature to 375°F (190°C). Lightly brush the bottom and sides of the Dutch oven with olive oil. Place a single layer of the eggplant slices on the bottom of the pot. Spread one-fourth of the meat sauce on top. Repeat with four more layers of eggplant and three more layers of meat sauce, ending with the eggplant. Pour the béchamel sauce on top and sprinkle with the remaining 3 tablespoons (18 g) of cheese.

Transfer the pot to the oven and bake until the moussaka is browned and bubbly on top, about 40 minutes. Remove from the oven and sprinkle with the remaining 1 tablespoon (4 g) of parsley. Let the moussaka rest for 20 minutes before serving.

Sicilian Sea Bass in Tomatoes with Fried Capers

Set in the heart of the Mediterranean, Sicily is celebrated for its vibrant cuisine, especially dishes highlighting the island's abundant seafood like swordfish, tuna, and sardines. Here, sea bass takes on a distinctly Sicilian character, paired with slow-roasted tomatoes and bell peppers, crisp fried capers, and a generous drizzle of fruity extra-virgin olive oil.

MAKES 4 SERVINGS

3 tablespoons (45 ml) canola oil

¼ cup (35 g) capers, drained

3½ cups (525 g) cherry tomatoes

1 red bell pepper, seeded and chopped

1 small yellow onion, diced

5 garlic cloves, thinly sliced

1 cup (240 ml) extra-virgin olive oil, plus more for drizzling

Kosher salt and freshly ground pepper

1 teaspoon dried oregano

4 skin-on sea bass or halibut fillets, each about 5 ounces (150 g)

8 fresh oregano sprigs

1 lemon

Fresh basil leaves, for garnish

In a small frying pan over medium-high heat, warm the canola oil. Carefully add half of the capers (they will spatter). Fry, swirling the pan to move the capers around, until they are golden brown, about 1 minute. Using a slotted spoon, transfer the capers to a paper towel-lined plate. Repeat to fry the remaining capers and set aside.

Preheat the oven to 400°F (200°C).

In a 9-by-13-inch (23 by 33 cm) ceramic baking dish, combine the tomatoes, bell pepper, onion, garlic, olive oil, a generous pinch of salt, a few grinds of pepper, and dried oregano. Stir to coat the vegetables with the oil. Bake until the tomatoes have burst and the red peppers and onions have softened, 35 to 40 minutes.

Arrange the fish, skin side down, in the baking dish in a single layer, nestling them in the tomato mixture and spacing them evenly. Drizzle the fish with olive oil and season with salt and pepper. Top each fillet with 1 of the oregano sprigs. Bake until the fish is just opaque throughout when tested with the tip of a knife, 10 to 15 minutes, depending on the thickness of the fillets.

Finely grate some lemon zest on each fillet and squeeze a little lemon juice on top. Scatter the remaining oregano sprigs and basil leaves on the fish, top with the fried capers, and serve immediately.

Chinese-Style Whole Fish with Ginger and Chile Crisp

Growing up, Williams Sonoma test kitchen chef Lena Wu often found her father—also a chef—preparing this traditional Chinese-style whole fish, a beloved dish for Lunar New Year celebrations. Simple, flavorful, and steeped in nostalgia, it's the kind of recipe that always resonates. Lena gives it a personal twist with a generous spoonful of her homemade chile crisp. We like to make it with branzino, but red snapper, mahi-mahi, or grouper work just as well.

MAKES 2 SERVINGS

1 whole branzino, about 1 pound (450 g), cleaned, with head and tail intact

¾ teaspoon kosher salt

2 teaspoons peeled and grated fresh ginger, plus 5 thin slices

2 green onions, 1 halved lengthwise and 1 thinly sliced on the diagonal

7 tablespoons (105 ml) avocado oil

2 garlic cloves, thinly sliced

1 tablespoon (15 ml) tamari

Fresh cilantro leaves, for garnish (optional)

2 cups (310 g) cooked brown or white rice

Lena's Chile Crisp (page 138)

Preheat the oven to 450°F (230°C).

Pat the fish dry with paper towels. Using a large, sharp knife, make three diagonal cuts on each side of the fish, running vertically from fin to belly and slicing deep enough to hit the bones. Season the skin and cavity with the salt. Stuff the cavity with the sliced ginger and halved green onion.

In a large, nonstick ovenproof frying pan just big enough for the fish, heat 2 tablespoons (30 ml) of the avocado oil over medium-high heat until it shimmers. Add the fish and sear until browned and crisp, 3 to 4 minutes on each side. Turn the fish so the belly (cut side) is down and the fish is upright; you may need to press down gently to flatten the belly. Wipe out any excess oil from the pan.

Transfer the pan to the oven and roast the fish until just cooked through, about 5 minutes. Transfer the fish to a serving platter on its side and return the pan to the stovetop. Scatter the grated ginger and half of the sliced green onion over the top of the fish. Set the platter near the stove.

Wipe out the pan and turn the heat to medium-high. Add the remaining 5 tablespoons (75 ml) of oil and the garlic to the pan. Cook until the edges of the garlic have turned golden brown, about 45 seconds. Remove from the heat and immediately pour the hot garlic oil over the fish. (This will help cook the raw ginger and green onion, and you should hear a nice sizzle.) Drizzle with the tamari and top with the rest of the sliced green onion and the cilantro, if using.

Serve immediately with the rice and chile crisp alongside.

Lena's Chile Crisp

Williams Sonoma test kitchen chef Lena Wu's condiment combines her favorite aromatics with two types of chile flakes: classic red pepper flakes and Korean gochugaru, which lends sweetness, smokiness, and a peppery kick. Find gochugaru in Asian markets or online. The recipe makes extra fried shallots and garlic—perfect for sprinkling over other dishes.

MAKES 1 CUP (240 G)

SHALLOT AND GARLIC CRISPS

3 medium shallots

6 large garlic cloves

1 cup (240 ml) neutral oil, such as avocado

2 green onions, white and green parts separated and sliced

3-inch (7.5 cm) piece fresh ginger, peeled and halved lengthwise

2 orange peel strips, each 3 to 4 inches (7.5 to 10 cm) long, preferably Valencia

1 tablespoon (8 g) Sichuan peppercorns

2 star anise pods

1 cinnamon stick

1 bay leaf

To make the shallot and garlic crisps: Using a mandoline, thinly slice the shallots crosswise into rings and the garlic cloves lengthwise, preferably no more than 1⁄16 inch (2 mm) thick. Set aside.

Set a fine-mesh sieve over a heatproof bowl with a pouring spout or a large 4-cup (960 ml) glass measuring cup; set aside. Line a rimmed baking sheet with paper towels and set aside.

In a 4-quart (3.6 L) saucepan, heat the oil over medium-high heat for 2 minutes. Add the shallots, which will begin to sizzle, decrease the heat to medium-low, and simmer, stirring continuously around the edges of the saucepan with wooden chopsticks or a wooden spoon, until light golden brown, 6 to 10 minutes. Immediately pour the shallots and oil into the fine-mesh sieve. Drain the shallots thoroughly, then transfer them to the prepared baking sheet, spreading them out so they don't stick together as they cool. Return the oil to the saucepan and return the sieve to over the bowl.

Return the pan to medium heat and warm the oil. Add the sliced garlic. When it begins to sizzle, decrease the heat to medium-low and fry, stirring occasionally, until medium golden brown, about 3 minutes. Immediately pour the garlic and oil into the fine-mesh sieve.

Scatter the garlic next to the fried shallots on the prepared baking sheet. Return the oil to the saucepan and return the sieve to over the bowl.

POUR-OVER INGREDIENTS

5 scant tablespoons (25 g) gochugaru Korean pepper flakes

3 tablespoons (12 g) red pepper flakes

1 tablespoon (12 g) sugar

2 teaspoons mushroom bouillon powder

1 teaspoon salt

1 teaspoon tamari or low-sodium soy sauce

Return the pan to medium heat and warm the oil. Add the green onions, ginger, orange peels, Sichuan peppercorns, star anise pods, cinnamon stick, and bay leaf. Once the aromatics begin to sizzle, decrease the heat to low and simmer, stirring occasionally, to infuse for 30 minutes; watch carefully and adjust the heat to maintain a gentle simmer. If any of the ingredients begins to burn, such as the orange peel or green part of the green onions, remove those ingredients and continue simmering.

Meanwhile, to make the pour-over ingredients: In a medium heatproof bowl, combine the gochugaru, red pepper flakes, sugar, mushroom bouillon powder, and salt.

When the aromatics have finished simmering, pour the contents of the pan into the fine-mesh sieve, then discard the contents of the sieve. Let the oil cool to 280°F (138°C) on an instant-read thermometer. If the oil is not warm enough, return it to the saucepan and heat gently. Pour the oil over the gochugaru mixture and stir to combine. Let stand for 15 minutes to allow the ingredients to infuse.

Meanwhile, finely crush 2 tablespoons (20 g) of the fried garlic with the flat bottom of a measuring cup. Transfer to a bowl and add 2 tablespoons (20 g) of uncrushed garlic. Finely crush ¼ cup (25 g) of the fried shallots and combine with the garlic. The remaining fried garlic and shallots can be stored in an airtight container at room temperature for up to 1 week.

Stir the tamari into the gochugaru-oil mixture, then add the garlic-shallot mixture and stir again. Transfer to an airtight jar and store at room temperature for up to 1 month. Serve on anything and everything.

Layered Chicken Three-Cheese Enchilada

Choose your favorite enchilada sauce for this comforting casserole, which layers tender corn tortillas with shredded chicken and a trio of cheeses. Baked until bubbling and golden, it's a hearty dish that's perfect for feeding a hungry crowd. Serve it hot with a sprinkle of fresh cilantro or a dollop of sour cream for a finishing touch.

MAKES 6 SERVINGS

1 tablespoon (15 ml) olive oil

1 yellow onion, cut into ½-inch (13 mm) dice

Kosher salt and freshly ground pepper

1¼ pounds (565 g) boneless, skinless chicken breasts, cooked and shredded

1¾ cups (420 ml) red enchilada sauce

9 corn tortillas, each about 6 inches (15 cm) in diameter

¾ cup (90 g) shredded mozzarella cheese

¾ cup (90 g) shredded white cheddar cheese

¾ cup (90 g) shredded yellow cheddar cheese

Sliced green onion tops, for garnish

Chopped fresh cilantro, for garnish

Preheat the oven to 350°F (180°C).

In a large nonstick sauté pan over medium-high heat, warm the olive oil. Add the onion, season with salt and pepper, and cook, stirring occasionally, until the onion is soft, 6 to 7 minutes. Remove from the heat and let cool.

Add the chicken to the onion and stir well to combine.

Spread ¼ cup (60 ml) of the enchilada sauce on the bottom of a 3½-quart (3.1 L) round wide Dutch oven. Arrange 3 tortillas in a single layer on the sauce, overlapping them as needed to cover the sauce. Top with a generous 1 cup (140 g) of the chicken-onion mixture, ½ cup (120 ml) of the sauce, and ¼ cup (30 g) of each cheese. Repeat the layering two more times, alternating the direction of the tortilla layers and finishing with ½ cup (120 ml) of sauce and ¼ cup (30 g) of each cheese.

Transfer to the oven and bake until the ingredients are heated through and the cheese is melted, about 30 minutes. Remove from the oven and garnish with green onions and cilantro.

Korean-Style Grilled Short Ribs with Gochujang Peanut Sauce

For a fun Father's Day twist, trade steaks for these Korean-inspired short ribs. Sliced Hasselback style, the meat soaks up a bold marinade of ginger, garlic, soy sauce, and gochugaru (or red pepper flakes). A spicy-sweet peanut sauce spiked with gochujang rounds out the dish. Serve the grilled ribs with lettuce leaves, cucumbers, scallions, and other garnishes so everyone can build their own lettuce cups. Boneless short ribs are ideal, but tri-tip works too.

MAKES 4 TO 6 SERVINGS

SHORT RIBS

2 pounds (1 kg) boneless beef short ribs, 1 to 1½ inches (2.5 to 4 cm) thick

½ cup (120 ml) soy sauce

¼ cup (60 ml) seasoned rice vinegar

3 tablespoons (45 ml) toasted sesame oil

¼ cup (55 g) firmly packed dark brown sugar

2 tablespoons (30 g) gochugaru

1 heaping tablespoon (6 g) grated garlic

1 heaping tablespoon (6 g) grated fresh ginger

To make the short ribs: Using a sharp knife, slice the ribs on the diagonal every ¼ inch (6 mm), making sure not to cut all the way through (this is called a Hasselback cut).

In a large bowl, whisk together the soy sauce, vinegar, sesame oil, brown sugar, gochugaru, garlic, and ginger. Add the short ribs and turn to coat with the marinade, then submerge them in the marinade. Cover the bowl with plastic wrap and refrigerate overnight.

Continued on page 144

Continued from page 143

GOCHUJANG PEANUT SAUCE

½ cup (130 g) smooth peanut butter

3 to 4 tablespoons (45 to 60 g) gochujang, depending on desired spice level

3 tablespoons (45 ml) soy sauce

3 tablespoons (45 ml) maple syrup

2 tablespoons (30 ml) warm water

1 tablespoon (10 ml) toasted sesame oil

Juice of 1 lime

2 garlic cloves, grated

2 teaspoons grated fresh ginger

Kosher salt

Vegetable oil, as needed

1 head butter lettuce, leaves separated

2 Persian cucumbers, cut into matchsticks

Halved limes, for serving

1 bunch scallions, sliced on the diagonal

White and black sesame seeds, for garnish

To make the gochujang peanut sauce: In a medium bowl, combine the peanut butter, gochujang, soy sauce, maple syrup, warm water, sesame oil, lime juice, garlic, and ginger and stir until smooth. You can make the sauce in advance; cover and refrigerate, then bring to room temperature before serving.

When ready to cook, remove the short ribs from the refrigerator and transfer them to a baking sheet or platter, reserving the marinade. Season the ribs lightly with salt. Pour the marinade into a small saucepan, place over medium-high heat, and bring to a boil. Decrease the heat and simmer until thickened slightly, about 5 minutes. Remove from the heat and cover to keep warm.

Prepare a medium-hot fire in a grill or heat a cast-iron skillet or grill pan over medium-high heat. Oil the grill grates or pan.

Arrange the short ribs on the grill or in the pan. Cook, turning the ribs once halfway through, until a deeply browned, caramelized crust forms and the meat that's visible between the Hasselback cuts is mostly cooked through, with just a bit of pink showing, 4 to 5 minutes total for smaller ribs and 8 to 10 minutes total for larger ribs.

Transfer the ribs to a platter along with the lettuce leaves, cucumbers, limes, and gochujang peanut sauce. Sprinkle the ribs with the scallions and sesame seeds. Serve the reduced marinade as a sauce alongside the short ribs.

Acorn Squash Dal with Cashew-Cilantro Rice

Dal—a spiced lentil purée that varies from region to region—is a cornerstone of Indian cooking. In this version, hearty chunks of acorn squash are folded in, and it's served with cashew-cilantro rice for a comforting vegetarian meal. Like it hot? Simply add more cayenne to turn up the heat.

MAKES 4 SERVINGS

DAL

2 tablespoons (30 ml) vegetable oil

1 yellow onion, finely chopped

2 garlic cloves, minced

1 teaspoon ground cumin

1 teaspoon ground coriander

¼ teaspoon cayenne pepper

1 acorn squash, peeled, seeded, and cut into 1½-inch (4 cm) cubes

One 14-ounce (420 g) can crushed tomatoes

1 dried red chile

1 cup (220 g) dried red lentils

4 cups (960 ml) water

Kosher salt and freshly ground pepper

RICE

2 tablespoons (30 g) ghee or unsalted butter

2 garlic cloves, minced

½ teaspoon ground turmeric

½ teaspoon ground cumin

½ teaspoon kosher salt

2 cups (440 g) basmati rice

3 cups (720 ml) water

1 bay leaf

½ cup (75 g) coarsely chopped toasted cashews

½ cup (15 g) fresh cilantro leaves

To make the dal: In a Balti dish or deep sauté pan over medium heat, warm the vegetable oil. Add the onion and sauté until softened, about 3 minutes. Add the garlic, cumin, coriander, and cayenne and cook, stirring frequently, until fragrant, about 2 minutes. Add the squash, tomatoes, dried chile, lentils, water, and a pinch of salt; stir to combine. Bring to a boil, then decrease the heat to a simmer. Simmer, uncovered, until the squash and lentils are tender, about 30 minutes.

While the dal is cooking, make the rice: In a saucepan or Dutch oven over medium heat, melt the ghee. Add the garlic and cook, stirring, until fragrant, about 30 seconds. Add the turmeric, cumin, and salt and cook until fragrant, about 30 seconds more. Add the rice and stir to coat with the butter and spices. Cook, stirring occasionally, until the rice is toasted, about 3 minutes. Add the water and the bay leaf and cover the pan. Bring to a boil, then decrease the heat to a simmer and cook, covered, for 20 minutes. Remove from the heat and let stand, covered, for 10 minutes. Remove the lid, fluff the rice with a fork, and stir in the cashews and cilantro.

To serve, remove the dried chile from the dal and discard. Divide the dal and rice among individual plates and serve immediately.

Chuck Williams's Clams Algarve

In the late 1970s, Chuck Williams traveled to Portugal and discovered the cataplana, a copper clamshell pot used for cooking seafood from the Algarve. He later adapted this simple method for clams—easily done in a Dutch oven or heavy saucepan. This recipe, along with many of his favorites, appears in our limited-edition Cooking at Home *honoring his 100th birthday.*

MAKES 4 TO 6 SERVINGS

3 pounds (1.4 kg) small clams, well-scrubbed

2 tablespoons (30 ml) olive oil

2 yellow onions, thinly sliced

Dash of hot pepper sauce

Salt and freshly ground pepper

2 to 3 ounces (60 to 90 g) smoked ham, cut into matchsticks

2 to 3 ounces (60 to 90 g) Spanish-style cured chorizo, thinly sliced

1 cup (240 ml) dry white wine

1 tablespoon (4 g) chopped fresh flat-leaf parsley

Discard any open clams that do not close to the touch. Set aside.

In a heavy saucepan over medium-low heat, warm the olive oil. When the oil is hot, add the onions, hot pepper sauce, and salt and pepper to taste and sauté until the onions are translucent, 7 to 10 minutes. Do not allow the onions to brown.

Add the ham, chorizo, and wine. Cover, decrease the heat to low, and cook gently for about 15 minutes to blend the flavors. Raise the heat to medium-high, add the clams, and scatter the parsley over the clams. Cover tightly and cook, shaking the pan occasionally and tossing the clams once or twice, until the clams open, about 5 minutes.

Discard any clams that did not open during cooking. Using a slotted spoon, transfer the clams to warmed soup plates or bowls. Spoon the broth, together with the ham and sausage, over the top of the clams. Serve immediately.

CHUCK'S TIP

Any heavy saucepan will work well. This is delicious served with crusty French bread.

LE CREUSET

Vietnamese Fresh Spring Rolls

Thought to have originated in China, spring rolls were traditionally enjoyed to mark the arrival of spring. In our take on this classic, we fill delicate rice papers with thin slices of carrot, purple radish, and cucumber, then wrap slender cucumber ribbons around the outside for an elegant touch.

MAKES 10 SPRING ROLLS

SPRING ROLLS

3 carrots, peeled

1 purple radish, peeled

2 English cucumbers, peeled

4 ounces (120 g) thin dried rice noodles, prepared according to package instructions

½ cup (15 g) fresh cilantro leaves

10 large round rice papers

SWEET CHILE DIPPING SAUCE

¼ cup (60 ml) seasoned rice vinegar

¼ cup (60 ml) hot water

2 tablespoons (24 g) sugar

1 tablespoon (15 ml) fish sauce

1 teaspoon chile paste, such as sambal oelek

Roy Choi's Pinch of LA Seasoning or sesame seeds, for garnish

To make the spring rolls: Using a julienne peeler, julienne the carrots and radish. Using a spiralizer fitted with the angel hair shredder, spiralize 1 of the cucumbers. Fit the spiralizer with the flat blade and spiralize the remaining cucumber into wide, thin ribbons.

Wrap a cutting board with plastic wrap to make rolling the filled rice papers easier. Arrange the vegetables, rice noodles, and cilantro next to the board and have ready a wide, shallow bowl filled with warm water.

Soak 1 of the rice papers in the warm water until just pliable, 10 to 15 seconds. Carefully remove the wrapper from the bowl and place it flat on the cutting board.

Add a small handful of the rice noodles, thinly shredded cucumber, carrot, radish, and cilantro leaves to the middle of the wrapper. Gently pull the closest edge of the rice paper toward you and then pull and roll it over the filling. Tuck the filling tightly into the rice paper and roll it over once to secure it. Then fold over the sides to close the ends of the roll. Continue rolling the spring roll over itself until fully sealed. Transfer to a platter. Repeat with the remaining rice papers and fillings.

Place one of the cucumber ribbons on your cutting board, with a short end facing you. Place one of the spring rolls crosswise on top of the cucumber at the end closest to you. Roll the spring roll and cucumber together so that cucumber ribbon covers most of the rice paper. Place the spring roll back on the platter, seam side down. Repeat with the remaining spring rolls and cucumber ribbons.

To make the sweet chile dipping sauce: In a small bowl, whisk together the vinegar, hot water, sugar, fish sauce, and chile paste until the sugar is dissolved.

Sprinkle the spring rolls with Pinch of LA Seasoning and serve with the dipping sauce alongside.

Miso Soup with Black Cod and Green Onions

This elegant soup is an ideal light supper for a warm summer night. Present it in shallow bowls to highlight the caramelized black cod, its golden crust gleaming against the broth. Pair it with a chilled seaweed or sesame-spinach salad and consider a crisp white wine to complete the meal.

MAKES 2 SERVINGS

3 cups (720 ml) cold water

3-inch (7.5 cm) piece kombu

½ cup 15 g) bonito flakes

2 tablespoons (30 g) white miso paste

5 ounces (150 g) black cod, cut into 2 or 4 pieces

1 tablespoon (15 ml) olive oil

Kosher salt and freshly ground pepper

1 green onion, white and tender green parts, thinly sliced

Put the cold water and kombu in a saucepan over medium heat. Bring to a boil and then remove and discard the kombu. Turn off the heat, add the bonito flakes, gently stir once, and let sit for 5 minutes. Strain the soup through a fine-mesh sieve and return the broth to the saucepan.

Put the miso paste in a small bowl and add ¼ cup (60 ml) of the warm broth. Stir until the mixture is very smooth. Add the miso mixture to the saucepan and warm gently, taking care not to let the soup come to a boil.

Place a small frying pan over high heat until it is very hot. Rub the cod with the oil and season with salt and pepper. Sear until just cooked through, about 4 minutes per side.

To serve, ladle the soup into bowls, top with 1 or 2 pieces of fish, and sprinkle with the green onions.

The Grill Master's Kitchen

Grilling Meat and Veggies

Grilling is where technique meets instinct. Unlike the controlled environment of an indoor kitchen, outdoor cooking demands that you read the fire, understand your ingredients, and trust your senses. When you nail the perfect sear on Grilled Rib-Eye Steaks with Herb Butter (page 154) or achieve that ideal balance of char and tenderness in Barbecued Baby Back Ribs (page 159), you're experiencing cooking at its most elemental and satisfying.

Grilled Rib-Eye Steaks with Herb Butter

This classic steak preparation gets a twist from a blend of multicolored peppercorns: black, white, pink, and green. To achieve the coarse texture you need, seal the peppercorns in a plastic bag and crush them with a rolling pin, a meat mallet, or the bottom of a heavy pan.

MAKES 4 SERVINGS

4 boneless rib-eye steaks, each 12 to 14 ounces (360 to 420 g) and about 1 inch (2.5 cm) thick

Kosher salt

½ cup (60 g) coarsely crushed mixed peppercorns

Herb Butter (this page), for serving

Prepare a grill for direct high heat (about 450°F to 500°F/230°C to 260°C). If using a gas grill, preheat all burners on high for 10 to 15 minutes. If using a charcoal grill, build a hot fire and let the coals burn until covered with white ash. Clean and oil the grill grates.

Season the steaks with salt, then generously sprinkle the crushed peppercorns on both sides of each steak, pressing them so they adhere. Grill the steaks, turning once, until well-marked and cooked to medium-rare, 4 to 5 minutes per side, or until cooked to your liking. Transfer to a serving board and let rest for 5 to 10 minutes before serving.

Top each steak with a generous dollop of Herb Butter below and serve immediately.

Herb Butter

A simple but delicious embellishment for grilled rib-eye steaks, compound butter is a blend of butter and fresh herbs.

MAKES 4 SERVINGS

3 tablespoons (45 g) unsalted butter, at room temperature

2 tablespoons (4 g) snipped fresh chives

1 tablespoon (4 g) minced fresh rosemary

Kosher salt and freshly ground pepper

In a small dish, stir together the butter, chives, rosemary, and a pinch each of salt and pepper. Shape the butter into a log, wrap tightly in parchment paper or plastic wrap, and refrigerate for up to 1 week or freeze for up to 3 months.

Grilled Lobster with Lemon Butter

This simple recipe is all you need to enjoy delicious grilled lobster. We use a Traeger grill for a hint of smoky flavor. Visit your local fishmonger for fresh lobster tails, and if you have any extra lemon butter, serve it with grilled, crusty bread.

MAKES 4 SERVINGS

- 1 cup (240 g) unsalted butter, cut into 1-inch (2.5 cm) cubes
- 4 garlic cloves, grated
- Zest and juice of 1 lemon
- Pinch of cayenne pepper
- Kosher salt and freshly ground pepper
- 8 lobster tails or 4 live lobsters
- 2 lemons, halved crosswise
- Flaky sea salt, for sprinkling
- ⅓ cup (20 g) minced fresh flat-leaf parsley

In a small ovenproof pot, combine the butter, garlic, lemon zest and juice, and cayenne; season with salt and black pepper. Set aside.

To prepare live lobsters (if using): Parboil the lobsters in boiling water for 8 to 10 minutes until shells turn red. Let cool slightly, then split each lobster in half lengthwise. Remove and discard the stomach sac and intestinal vein. Rinse, pat dry, and proceed with grilling.

To prepare lobster tails (if using): Using kitchen shears or a sharp knife, cut the tails down the middle. Rinse each tail in cold water, then remove the intestinal vein and the tomalley. Using your hands, split open the cut tail and carefully place the lobster meat on top of the tail. Transfer the lobster tails to a baking sheet and pat dry. Set aside.

Set the temperature on a Traeger wood pellet grill to 450°F (230°C), close the lid, and preheat according to the manufacturer's instructions.

Place the pot with the butter mixture on the grill and close the lid. Let the butter melt, 7 to 8 minutes. Stir to combine the ingredients, then, using an oven mitt, move the pot to one side of the grill, keeping the pot on the grill.

Place the lobster tails, cut sides up, on the grill grate. Brush the meat with some of the lemon butter. Place the lemon halves, cut sides down, on the grill. Close the lid and cook until an instant-read thermometer inserted into the lobster meat registers 140°F (60°C), about 10 minutes; the shells should be red and the meat should be opaque throughout but still moist when tested with the tip of a knife.

Transfer the lobster tails and lemon halves to a platter. Using the oven mitt, remove the pot with the remaining butter from the grill. Using a clean brush, brush the lobster meat with more lemon butter. Garnish with a sprinkling of flaky sea salt, the parsley, and a fresh squeeze of lemon juice. Serve immediately with the remaining lemon butter alongside.

Honey-Lime Grilled Chicken

A sweet and zesty marinade gives this grilled chicken a punch of bright, balanced flavor. It's a simple recipe for a delicious, crowd-pleasing weeknight dinner.

MAKES 4 SERVINGS

MARINADE

¼ cup (60 g) honey

¼ cup (60 ml) fresh lime juice

3 tablespoons (45 ml) soy sauce

3 garlic cloves, minced

CHICKEN

4 boneless, skinless chicken breasts or 8 boneless, skinless chicken thighs

Chopped fresh cilantro, for garnish (optional)

To make the marinade: In a bowl, whisk together the honey, lime juice, soy sauce, and minced garlic.

To make the chicken: Place the chicken in a large resealable bag or a dish. Pour half of the marinade over the chicken, making sure it's fully coated. Reserve the remaining marinade to use as a glaze later. Seal the bag or cover the dish and refrigerate for at least 30 minutes or up to 2 hours.

Preheat your grill to medium-high heat. Lightly oil the grates.

Remove the chicken from the marinade and place it on the grill. Cook for 6 to 8 minutes per side, or until the chicken is cooked through and has a nice char. The internal temperature should reach 165°F (74°C).

During the last few minutes of cooking, brush the reserved marinade over the chicken.

Remove the chicken from the grill and let it rest for a few minutes. Garnish with fresh cilantro, if desired. Serve immediately.

Barbecued Baby Back Ribs

For the best of both worlds, these baby back ribs are cooked low and slow in the oven before finishing on the grill for a smoky flavor. This two-step method is also convenient: you can cook the ribs in advance and quickly grill them after your guests arrive. For an even smokier flavor, use your grill's smoking box.

MAKES 6 SERVINGS

RUB

½ cup (115 g) brown sugar

2 tablespoons (16 g) chili powder

2 teaspoons kosher salt

1 teaspoon smoked paprika

2 racks baby back ribs, about 5 pounds (2.3 kg) total

BARBECUE SAUCE

¾ cup (180 ml) ketchup

¼ cup (55 g) brown sugar

2 tablespoons (30 ml) Worcestershire sauce

¼ cup (60 ml) apple cider

1 tablespoon (15 ml) soy sauce

1 tablespoon (15 ml) Dijon mustard

1 teaspoon onion powder

1 teaspoon garlic powder

½ teaspoon ground cinnamon

Pinch of ground nutmeg

Large pinch of kosher salt

Preheat the oven to 325°F (170°C). Line a rimmed baking sheet with aluminum foil.

To make the rub: In a small bowl, stir together the brown sugar, chili powder, salt, and paprika.

Place the ribs on the prepared baking sheet and spread the rub evenly over both sides of the ribs. Transfer the ribs to the oven and cook, turning the ribs every hour, until the meat starts to pull away from the bones, about 3 hours. Remove the ribs from the oven and let rest for at least 10 minutes or up to 1 hour. At this point the ribs can be finished on the grill or refrigerated up to overnight, if desired. If refrigerated, remove the ribs from the refrigerator about 1 hour before grilling to allow them to come to room temperature.

To make the barbecue sauce: In a saucepan, combine the ketchup, brown sugar, Worcestershire sauce, apple cider, soy sauce, mustard, onion powder, garlic powder, cinnamon, nutmeg, and salt. Bring to a boil over medium-high heat, then decrease the heat to medium. Simmer the sauce until reduced by half, 4 to 5 minutes. Remove from the heat.

Prepare a hot fire in a grill. Place a steel grill roaster in the center of the grill, cover the grill, and preheat for 5 minutes.

Working in batches if necessary, place the ribs, meaty side down, on the grill pan and cook just until the fat starts to sizzle, 2 to 3 minutes. Turn the ribs over and cook for 2 to 3 minutes more. Transfer to a cutting board and baste with the barbecue sauce. Cut between the ribs to separate them and serve hot with the remaining barbecue sauce alongside.

Grilled Sausages and Cipollini Onions with Alabama BBQ Sauce

In honor of her father, award-winning chef Todd English, Belle English, Williams Sonoma's test kitchen culinary director, created this easy grilled sausage recipe for Father's Day. The dish features sausages and sweet cipollini onions, which were a favorite at her childhood home. For dipping, she serves an Alabama BBQ sauce inspired by her father's Las Vegas restaurant, The Beast. She loves the sauce's "evolved ranch dressing" flavor and believes it goes well with everything.

MAKES 8 SERVINGS

SAUSAGES AND ONIONS

12 ounces (360 g) cipollini onions, peeled

Extra-virgin olive oil, as needed

Kosher salt

1½ pounds (680 g) assorted sausages

ALABAMA BBQ SAUCE

1 cup (240 ml) mayonnaise

¼ cup (60 ml) apple cider vinegar

3 tablespoons (40 g) firmly packed dark brown sugar

1 tablespoon (15 g) Dijon mustard

¼ teaspoon cayenne pepper

Squeeze of fresh lemon juice

Kosher salt and freshly ground pepper

Whole-grain hot mustard, for serving

To make the sausages and onions: Prepare a medium-hot fire in a grill. Soak five bamboo or wooden skewers in water for 10 minutes, then drain.

In a large bowl, toss the onions with just enough olive oil to coat and season with salt. Thread the onions onto the skewers.

Place the sausages on the grill, spacing them about 2 inches (5 cm) apart, then arrange the onion skewers alongside. Close the lid and cook until the sausages are nicely grill-marked and the onions are charred and start to soften, 5 to 7 minutes. Turn the sausages and skewers over and cook until an instant-read thermometer inserted into the center of a sausage registers 165°F (74°C) and the onions are tender, about 7 minutes more. Transfer to a serving platter.

Meanwhile, to make the Alabama BBQ sauce: In a medium bowl, stir together the mayonnaise, vinegar, brown sugar, Dijon mustard, cayenne, and lemon juice until smooth. Season to taste with salt and black pepper.

Serve the sausages and onions with the BBQ sauce and hot mustard alongside.

Grilled Potato Salad with Scallions and Jalapeño

For a new take on a classic side, try this spicy potato salad with a smoky twist. We lightly char fingerling potatoes and jalapeño peppers on a grill to give them an extra layer of flavor. Halve the fingerlings lengthwise to maximize their smoky char, then toss them with the other ingredients, including a sprinkle of tangy sumac.

MAKES 4 SERVINGS

3 pounds (1.4 kg) fingerling potatoes

Kosher salt

⅔ cup (160 ml) extra-virgin olive oil

2 tablespoons (30 ml) cider vinegar

Juice of 1 lemon

2 garlic cloves

2 jalapeños

2 tablespoons (30 ml) avocado oil

Freshly ground pepper

2 bunches scallions, white and light green portions, thinly sliced on the diagonal

Leaves from 2 small bunches fresh flat-leaf parsley or cilantro

½ teaspoon sumac, plus more for garnish

Place the potatoes in a large pot and add cold water to cover. Season generously with salt, cover the pot, and bring to a boil over high heat. Uncover the pot and simmer until the potatoes are tender but not falling apart, 8 to 10 minutes. A paring knife inserted into the potatoes should meet no resistance.

Drain the potatoes, transfer to a rimmed baking sheet, and let cool for about 30 minutes.

While the potatoes are cooling, set the temperature on a Traeger wood pellet grill to 400°F (200°C), close the lid, and preheat according to the manufacturer's instructions for 15 minutes.

Meanwhile, in a large bowl, whisk together the olive oil, vinegar, and lemon juice. Grate the garlic into the vinaigrette and whisk to combine. Set aside.

When the potatoes are cool enough to handle, cut them in half lengthwise and return to the baking sheet, then add the jalapeños. Drizzle the potatoes and jalapeños with the avocado oil, season with salt and pepper, and toss to coat.

Place the potatoes, cut sides down, and the whole jalapeños on the grill and close the lid. Cook until the potatoes and jalapeños are nicely grill-marked underneath, about 10 minutes. Transfer to the baking sheet.

On a cutting board, thinly slice the jalapeños crosswise. Alternatively, cut them in half lengthwise, discarding the seeds if desired, then chop.

Add the potatoes, jalapeños, and scallions to the bowl with the vinaigrette. Using a rubber spatula, gently toss to combine. Add the parsley and sumac, season to taste with salt, and toss again.

Transfer the potato salad to a large serving platter and garnish with a large pinch of sumac. Serve warm or at room temperature.

Grilled Pork Chops with Caramelized Peaches and Basil

Grilling outside on a warm night calls for this quintessential dish. Sirloin chops, known for their intense pork flavor, are paired with two summer staples: sweet peaches and peppery basil. We grill the peaches after tossing them in maple syrup to help them caramelize, and a drizzle of balsamic vinegar adds a welcome acidic bite to the finished dish.

MAKES 4 SERVINGS

4 bone-in pork loin or end-loin chops, each about 9 ounces (270 g) and ¾ inch (2 cm) thick, trimmed of excess fat

Olive oil for brushing, plus 2 teaspoons

Kosher salt and freshly ground pepper

2 peaches, quartered and pitted

2 tablespoons (30 ml) maple syrup

2 to 3 teaspoons good-quality balsamic vinegar

Small fresh basil leaves, for garnish

Remove the pork chops from the refrigerator and let stand for 30 minutes.

Brush the chops very lightly with olive oil and season generously on both sides with salt and pepper.

In a bowl, combine the peaches, maple syrup, and the 2 teaspoons olive oil. Season with pepper and toss to coat evenly. Set aside.

Prepare a medium-hot fire in a grill or preheat a cast-iron grill pan on the stovetop over medium-high heat.

Place the chops on the grill rack over the hottest part of the fire or in the grill pan and cook until golden, about 2 minutes. Move the chops to a cooler part of the grill or decrease the heat and cook until the pork is firm and cooked through but not dry, 3 to 4 minutes more per side. Place the peaches over direct heat and sear, turning with tongs, until the cut sides are golden, 30 to 60 seconds total.

Transfer the chops and peaches to a platter and drizzle sparingly with the vinegar. Garnish with basil leaves and serve immediately.

Grilled Corn Three Ways

Upgrade your grilled corn on the cob with a selection of three savory toppings. After cooking, slather the ears with butter and add your favorite seasoning: a smoky paprika mix; an Italian blend of fresh herbs and Parmesan; or a Mexican combo of cilantro, chili powder, and cotija cheese. If you're hosting a crowd, offer all three options and let your guests customize their own corn.

MAKES 4 SERVINGS

4 ears of corn

PAPRIKA TOPPING

6 tablespoons (90 g) unsalted butter

2 teaspoons smoked paprika

Flaky sea salt

HERB AND PARMESAN TOPPING

4 tablespoons (60 g) unsalted butter

Kosher salt and freshly ground pepper

1 tablespoon (4 g) chopped fresh flat-leaf parsley

1 tablespoon (3 g) chopped fresh oregano

½ cup (50 g) grated Parmesan cheese

Pinch of red pepper flakes

Cut four pieces of butcher's twine, each about 10 inches (25 cm) long, and place in a bowl of water.

Remove the tough outer husks from the corn and discard. Carefully pull back the tender inner husks, leaving them attached, and gather them at the stem end. Remove the twine from the water, tie the husks tightly with the twine, and cut off the excess. Remove and discard the silks. Place the corn in a large bowl of water and soak for 10 minutes. This will help prevent the husks from burning during grilling.

Preheat a hot fire in a grill. Brush and oil the grill grates. Remove the corn from the water and pat dry with paper towels. Place the corn on the grill and cook, turning the ears about every 1 minute, until the kernels turn a shade darker and are lightly charred and tender, about 5 minutes total. Transfer the corn to a serving platter.

To make the paprika topping: Spread 1½ tablespoons (23 g) of butter on each ear. Sprinkle with the smoked paprika and flaky sea salt.

To make the herb and Parmesan topping: Spread 1 tablespoon (15 g) of butter on each ear. Sprinkle with salt and pepper, then with the parsley, oregano, and Parmesan. Finish with a pinch of red pepper flakes.

Continued on page 168

Continued from page 167

CILANTRO AND COTIJA CHEESE TOPPING

4 tablespoons (60 g) unsalted butter

Kosher salt and freshly ground pepper

Pinch of chili powder

1 tablespoon (3 g) chopped fresh cilantro

1 tablespoon (4 g) chopped fresh flat-leaf parsley

2 ounces (60 g) cotija cheese, crumbled

To make the cilantro and cotija cheese topping: Spread 1 tablespoon (15 g) of butter on each ear. Sprinkle with salt and pepper and the chili powder, then with the cilantro, parsley, and cotija.

CHUCK'S TIP

Seek out a good local source for fresh corn on the cob—a roadside stand, a produce shop, or a high-quality market. Time is of the essence because the sugars in corn begin changing to starch within 7 minutes of picking! Check the silks beneath the husks. If they look translucent and still slightly green, you can use the corn for this recipe. If the silks have turned brown, forget it.

Grilled Portobello Mushrooms with Salsa Verde

Large portobello mushrooms are a natural fit for the grill. To enhance their flavor, we give them a quick marinade in a savory salsa verde with fresh parsley, cilantro, and garlic. Then, we cook the mushrooms on an outdoor grill until they're tender. These grilled portobellos are the perfect side dish for grilled steak or chicken, and they also make a satisfying vegetarian burger when served on a toasted bun with your favorite condiments.

MAKES 4 TO 6 SERVINGS

¾ cup (20 g) chopped fresh flat-leaf parsley

3 tablespoons (10 g) chopped fresh cilantro

4 garlic cloves, minced

½ cup (120 ml) extra-virgin olive oil

⅓ cup (80 ml) red wine vinegar

Kosher salt and freshly ground pepper

4 to 6 large portobello mushrooms, stems trimmed and caps brushed clean

Canola oil, for brushing

In a large bowl, stir together the parsley, cilantro, garlic, olive oil, and vinegar and season with salt and pepper. Add the mushrooms and toss to coat. Let marinate at room temperature for 15 minutes.

Meanwhile, prepare a medium-hot fire in a grill. Lightly brush an outdoor frying pan with canola oil. Place the pan on the grill, close the grill, and preheat the pan for 10 minutes.

Remove the mushrooms from the marinade, reserving the marinade. Arrange the mushrooms in the preheated pan and cook, turning once, until tender, 3 to 4 minutes per side. Transfer the mushrooms to a platter and serve immediately with the reserved marinade alongside.

The Joy of Savory Baking

Loaves, Rolls, and Other Hearty Bakes

Few things are more rewarding than turning a handful of basic ingredients into a warm, fragrant loaf of bread. This chapter is an invitation to discover the simple alchemy of baking at home. From our Classic Sourdough Bread (page 176) to the pillowy Tomato Focaccia with Garlic Rosemary Oil (page 183) and the tender Perfect Popovers (page 172), these recipes will suit every mood. Whether you're kneading the dough by hand or simply letting time do the work, you'll experience the timeless satisfaction of pulling a warm, homemade loaf from the oven.

NOTE: Baking recipes in this book use weight measurements (grams) for accuracy and consistent results. We highly recommend using a kitchen scale for all bread and pastry recipes.

Perfect Popovers

Making moist, airy popovers with crisp, golden domes is easy with the right pan. Our aluminized-steel pan provides a quick burst of heat, which makes them rise dramatically, and the tapered, spaced-out cups promote perfect air circulation. For best results, simply avoid overfilling the cups and don't open the oven door while they bake. Popovers are a classic side for Thanksgiving, but they are equally delicious with breakfast, soups, or stews.

MAKES 12 SERVINGS

4 tablespoons (60 g) unsalted butter, melted

6 eggs, lightly beaten

2 cups (480 ml) milk

2 cups (280 g) all-purpose flour

1 teaspoon kosher salt

Unsalted butter, for serving (optional)

Preheat the oven to 450°F (230°C). Spray the wells of a standard 6-cup popover pan with nonstick cooking spray. Pour ½ teaspoon of the melted butter into each cup.

In a bowl, whisk together the eggs and milk, then whisk in 2 tablespoons (30 ml) of the melted butter.

In a large bowl, whisk together the flour and salt, then whisk in the egg mixture. Whisk vigorously until smooth, about 2 minutes. Divide the batter evenly among the 6 prepared cups, filling each cup about halfway or with 3/4 cup of batter. Bake for 20 minutes. Decrease the oven temperature to 325°F (170°C) and bake for 15 minutes more.

Remove from the oven and invert the pan onto a wire rack. Let the pan cool. Spray the walls again, add the remaining melted butter, and bake the remaining batter in the same 6-cup increments. Serve immediately with butter.

CHUCK'S TIP

To encourage the popovers to rise fully, use a pan with deep cups and heat it up in the preheated oven before you add the batter.

Rosemary-Lemon No-Knead Bread

This bread is almost effortless to make because it requires no kneading. The dough slowly rises over time and then bakes in a preheated, covered Dutch oven. This simple process creates a delicious loaf with a perfectly crispy, bakery-style crust.

MAKES ONE 1½-POUND (680 G) LOAF, 12 SERVINGS

3 cups (420 g) all-purpose flour, plus more as needed

¼ teaspoon instant yeast

1¾ teaspoons salt

2 teaspoons chopped fresh rosemary

2 teaspoons chopped lemon zest

Cornmeal, as needed

In a large bowl, combine the flour, yeast, salt, rosemary, and lemon zest. Add 1½ cups plus 2 tablespoons (13 fl. oz./410 ml) water and stir until blended; the dough will be shaggy and very sticky. Cover the bowl with plastic wrap. Let the dough rest at warm room temperature (about 70°F [21°C]) until the surface is dotted with bubbles, 12 to 18 hours.

Place the dough on a lightly floured work surface. Sprinkle the dough with a little flour and fold the dough over onto itself once or twice. Cover loosely with plastic wrap and let rest for 15 minutes.

Using just enough flour to keep the dough from sticking to the work surface or your fingers, gently and quickly shape the dough into a ball. Generously coat a cotton towel, preferably a flour sack towel (not terry cloth), with cornmeal. Put the dough, seam side down, on the towel and dust with more flour or cornmeal. Cover with another cotton towel and let rise until the dough is more than double in size and does not readily spring back when poked with a finger, about 2 hours.

At least 30 minutes before the dough is ready, put a 2¾-quart (2.5 L) bread pot or Dutch oven in the oven and preheat the oven to 450°F (230°C).

Carefully remove the pot from the oven. Slide your hand under the towel and turn the dough over, seam side up, into the pot; it may look like a mess, but that's okay. Shake the pan once or twice if the dough is unevenly distributed; it will straighten out as it bakes. If desired, using a very sharp knife, cut three shallow parallel slits in the top of the dough. Cover with the lid and bake for 30 minutes. Uncover and continue baking until the loaf is browned, 15 to 30 minutes more.

Transfer the pot to a wire rack and let cool for 10 minutes. Using oven mitts, turn the pot on its side and gently turn out the bread; it will release easily.

Classic Sourdough Bread

San Francisco sourdough is famous for its crisp crust, chewy texture, and tangy flavor. Inspired by Tartine's method, this recipe makes the process approachable for home bakers. With a little patience, you'll create a loaf that's as rewarding to bake as it is to eat.

MAKES 8 TO 10 SERVINGS

SOURDOUGH STARTER

50 grams all-purpose flour

50 grams rye flour

100 grams room-temperature filtered water (if the room is cold, heat the water to about 80°F [27°C] before using)

To save time, you can ask your local bakery if they have a starter you can purchase. They're generally happy to support home bread making! Be sure to ask when it was last fed, so you are able to seamlessly get it on your preferred feeding schedule.

For this recipe, make sure your water does not contain chlorine or chloramine; use bottled water if necessary. Don't entirely discard your starter after making this bread. Repeat the feeding process once more and then refrigerate until ready to use again. Feed the starter once a week while refrigerated. Remove from the fridge 3 days before baking and feed it on a regular schedule once more and the night before baking your bread. If you are making bread weekly, you can keep you starter at room temperature, feeding it daily and consistently for best results. There are lots of recipes that incorporate sourdough starter leftovers for added flavor, such as banana bread, focaccia, and waffles.

To make the sourdough starter (1 to 2 weeks before making bread): In a 1-quart (960 ml) glass jar, bowl, or other container, combine the all-purpose flour, rye flour, and water. Using a small rubber spatula or spoon, mix until no dry bits remain and the mixture resembles thick pancake batter. Cover the top of the container loosely with a lid, kitchen towel, or plastic wrap to prevent the batter from drying out but still allowing it to breathe. Place a rubber band around the jar to mark the starter's height, so you can see how much it has risen. Let stand at room temperature until the mixture begins to bubble, puff, and lighten in color, 2 to 3 days. These are all signs of wild yeast activity, which will ultimately become the leaven and add the classic sourdough flavor characteristics to your bread.

Continued on page 178

Continued from page 176

DAILY FEED

20 grams sourdough starter

50 grams all-purpose flour

50 grams rye flour

100 grams room-temperature water (if the room is cold, heat the water to about 80°F [27°C] before using)

To feed your starter: When your starter begins to show wild yeast activity, begin feeding it regularly at the same time each day. If you feed the starter predictably, it will act predictably, which is what you want when making sourdough. Choose a time that works for your schedule. A feeding means you are adding flour and water to a portion of the starter, which hosts wild yeast. The flour and water give the wild yeast the nutrients needed to thrive. You will discard a large percentage of the starter each time, but you can add that to other batters to enhance their flavor.

When the starter falls by about ½ inch (13 mm)–check the rubber band on the glass container–this is an indication that it's time to feed it again. Feeding times will vary depending on your room's temperature. For example, if it's hot outside, you may need to feed it twice in one day. Once your starter begins to act predictably, doubling in size with bubbles and a sour smell and then falling by ½ inch (13 mm), it's ready to use for bread making. This typically occurs after 5 to 7 days of consistent feeding.

To plan your baking: Eight to 12 hours before baking, feed your starter to get it ready for making the dough. This step is called "making the leaven." Depending on your feeding schedule, you may need to feed it twice in one day, which is fine. The point is to have your starter in a "mature" stage when you make the dough, i.e., bubbled, lightly doming on top, and sour smelling. We recommend doing this in the morning or at night before bed. To test whether the leaven is mature, gently add about 1 tablespoon (15 grams) of it to a glass of water. If it floats, it's mature and ready to leaven your bread.

To make the bread:

Step 1: Dough hydration (autolyse)
In a large bowl, whisk together the bread flour, 25 grams of the whole-wheat flour, and the rye flour. Pour in 350 grams of the warm water and,

BREAD

450 grams bread flour

50 grams whole-wheat flour, plus more for dusting

25 grams rye flour

360 grams warm water (90° to 110°F [32° to 43°C])

10 grams fine sea salt

100 grams mature sourdough starter (leaven)

25 grams rice flour, for dusting

using a rubber spatula, mix together until no dry bits remain. The dough will look messy and ragged. Cover loosely with a kitchen towel or plastic wrap and let stand at room temperature for 1 hour.

Step 2: Mix the dough
Uncover the bowl. Using your hands, gently pinch in the salt, mature starter, and the remaining 10 grams of warm water until combined. Pull the bottom of the dough out from underneath and then fold it over on top of itself. Transfer to a clean large bowl. Cover loosely with a kitchen towel or plastic wrap and set in a spot that's 75° to 80°F (24° to 27°C), ideally in a warm, sunny spot or in a turned-off oven with the light on. If it's colder, it may take longer to rise. Let the dough rest for 30 minutes.

Step 3: Folds and bulk fermentation
After the dough has rested for 30 minutes, lightly dip your hand in water (this helps with handling the dough) and dramatically pull one underside quadrant of the dough up and over the top of the dough to help build the dough's gluten strength. Repeat for each quadrant. Recover the dough and let it rest in a warm spot. Repeat this process every 30 minutes, four to six more times (2 to 3 hours total), until the dough looks 30 to 50 percent larger in volume and jiggles, with a slight doming and some visible air bubbles.

Step 4: Pre-shape and rest
When the dough is ready, transfer it to a work surface and lightly dust the dough with whole-wheat flour. Using a bench scraper, gently flip the dough over so the floured side is facing down. Lightly dip your hand in water and pull two of the bottom four corners up and over the dough, sealing them in the middle top of the dough round. Repeat on each side.

Continued on page 180

Continued from page 179

Flip the dough over so it is seam side down and cover with a kitchen towel. Let rest at room temperature for 30 minutes.

Step 5: Prepare the breadbasket
While the dough is resting, in a small bowl, whisk together the remaining 25 grams of whole-wheat flour and the rice flour. Use some of the mixture to generously flour a small breadbasket (we use an 8-inch [20 cm] basket) or line a medium bowl with a kitchen towel and generously flour the towel. Save the remaining flour mixture for step 8.

Step 6: Final shaping
Uncover the dough and lightly dust it again with whole-wheat flour. Using a bench scraper, gently flip the dough over so the floured side is facing down. Lightly dip your hand in water and pull two of the bottom four corners up and over the dough, sealing them in the middle top of the dough round. Repeat on each side. Flip the dough over so it is seam side down. Using your hands and using the surface as an anchor, pull the dough toward you to create a tightly rounded shape. Shift the dough and pull toward you again. This will help mold the dough into a smooth, tight round.

Step 7: Final proof
Using the bench scraper, gently flip the dough round over so it is seam side up and transfer to the floured breadbasket or towel-lined bowl, keeping the seam side up. Cover with a kitchen towel or plastic wrap and let the dough rest in the same warm spot, ideally 75° to 80°F (24° to 27°C) for 3 to 4 hours. If it's colder, it will be 5 to 6 hours; if warmer, 2 to 3 hours. You can also let the dough rest in its bowl in the refrigerator, with the dough wrapped with plastic wrap to prevent condensation, for 10 to 12 hours, which will help it develop more flavor. Bring to room

temperature before baking. To check whether your dough is ready to bake, gently press it with your finger; it should slowly spring back and there should be a barely perceptible depression, but not much. If it quickly springs back, give it more time. If it leaves a depression, the dough may be overproofed.

Step 8: Score and bake

About 30 minutes before your bread is ready, place a lidded Dutch oven in a cold oven and preheat the oven to 500°F (260°C). When your oven is heated and the dough is ready, lightly dust the exposed side of the dough with the reserved whole-wheat flour mixture. Line a small cutting board with parchment paper and place it, parchment side down, on your breadbasket. Quickly flip the bread over onto the parchment. Carefully but quickly remove the Dutch oven from the oven and remove the lid. Grab the corners of the parchment and transfer the dough, still on the parchment, to the pot. Using a sharp knife or blade, quickly score the top of the bread; we like to score an X or a slash with a slight curve to it, which will allow the bread to rise and expand. The Dutch oven will be hot, so take care during this step. Replace the lid and return the pot to the oven. Decrease the oven temperature to 450°F (230°C) and bake for 20 minutes. Remove the lid and bake uncovered until the bread is dark golden, 20 to 25 minutes longer. Transfer the bread from the Dutch oven to a cooling rack and test for doneness by lightly tapping the bottom of your loaf–it should sound hollow. Let cool for at least 1 hour before serving. This is important for the bread baking, as the proteins will continue to cook as the loaf cools.

Tomato Focaccia with Garlic Rosemary Oil

To get the most out of your focaccia, serve it as a main course with a tossed green salad. Alternatively, you can cut it into bite-size pieces and serve them as a starter. For extra flair, use different varieties and colors of cherry tomatoes.

MAKES 8 SERVINGS

6¼ cups (850 g) bread flour

2½ cups (600 ml) room-temperature water (70° to 74°F [21° to 23°C])

3 teaspoons sugar

½ cup (120 ml) warm water (95°F [35°C])

One ¼-ounce (7 g) package active dry yeast (2¼ teaspoons)

1½ tablespoons (23 g) kosher salt

10 tablespoons (150 ml) extra-virgin olive oil, plus more as needed

4 garlic cloves, thinly sliced

Leaves from 2 fresh rosemary sprigs

12 ounces (360 g) assorted cherry and grape tomatoes, halved through the stem end

Flaky sea salt

In the bowl of an electric mixer fitted with the dough hook, combine the flour, room-temperature water, and 1½ teaspoons of the sugar and beat on low speed until a shaggy dough forms, about 3 minutes, stopping the mixer to scrape down the dough hook and sides of the bowl as needed to incorporate all of the flour. Cover the bowl with a towel and let stand while preparing the yeast mixture.

In a small bowl, whisk together the warm water, yeast, and remaining 1½ teaspoons of sugar until combined. Let stand until foamy, about 5 minutes.

Remove the towel from the mixer bowl. With the mixer on low speed, add the yeast mixture and beat until the liquid is absorbed, about 1 minute. Add the kosher salt, increase the speed to medium, and beat until the dough is very elastic and sticky, about 5 minutes. It will pull away from the sides of the bowl but will remain attached to the dough hook and the bottom of the bowl.

Coat the inside of a large bowl with 3 tablespoons (45 ml) of the olive oil. Scrape the dough into the prepared bowl and turn to coat with the oil. Cover loosely with plastic wrap and let stand in a warm spot until doubled in size, about 2½ hours.

Line a rimmed baking sheet (about 18 by 13 inches [45 by 33 cm]) with a Silpat baking mat and brush with 2 tablespoons (30 ml) of the olive oil.

Continued on page 184

Continued from page 183

Fold the dough over itself twice in the bowl to deflate slightly. Transfer the dough to the prepared baking sheet. Using oiled hands, gently stretch the dough out to the edges and corners of the pan. If the dough springs back toward the center, cover with plastic wrap and let stand for 10 minutes, then repeat to stretch the dough. Cover the pan with oiled plastic wrap and refrigerate for at least 2 hours or up to overnight.

One hour before baking the focaccia, remove from the refrigerator and let stand in a warm spot for 1 hour. In a small bowl, stir together the remaining 5 tablespoons (75 ml) of olive oil, the garlic, and the rosemary; set aside.

Preheat the oven to 450°F (230°C).

Remove the plastic wrap from the pan. Using lightly oiled fingers, press your fingertips firmly into the dough to make deep dimples over the entire surface. Arrange the tomatoes on top, pressing them down slightly into the dough. Drizzle the dough with the garlic and rosemary oil. Sprinkle generously with flaky sea salt.

Bake until the focaccia is deep golden brown all over and the tomatoes have collapsed slightly, 20 to 25 minutes; halfway through baking, lightly drizzle the dough with extra-virgin olive oil.

Transfer the baking sheet to a wire rack and let the focaccia cool for 10 minutes. Cut into slices and serve warm or at room temperature.

Buttermilk Biscuits

Buttery, flaky biscuits are beloved for their crisp, golden exterior and tender interior. So easy to prepare that many Southern cooks make a fresh batch for every meal, they're the perfect accompaniment to a breakfast of fried eggs and grits or a hearty soup for lunch.

MAKES 8 BISCUITS

1 cup (140 g) all-purpose flour, plus more as needed

1 cup (140 g) cake flour

2 teaspoons baking powder

½ teaspoon baking soda

½ teaspoon kosher salt

6 tablespoons (90 g) chilled unsalted butter, plus more for serving

¾ cup (180 ml) buttermilk

Honey, for serving (optional)

Preheat the oven to 400°F (200°C). Have ready an ungreased rimmed baking sheet.

In a bowl, sift together the all-purpose and cake flours, baking powder, baking soda, and salt. Cut the butter into tablespoons and scatter over the flour mixture. Using a pastry blender or two knives, cut the butter into the flour mixture just until the mixture forms coarse crumbs the size of peas. Add the buttermilk and stir just until the dough comes together. Knead the dough a few times in the bowl.

Turn out the dough onto a lightly floured work surface. Using a light touch, pat out the dough into a round ¾ inch (2 cm) thick. Using a 2½-inch (6 cm) round biscuit cutter or cookie cutter, cut out as many rounds as possible. Place them 1 inch (2.5 cm) apart on the baking sheet. Gather up the dough scraps, pat them out again, cut out more dough rounds, and add them to the baking sheet. You should get 8 biscuits. Bake the biscuits until they have risen and are golden brown, 18 to 20 minutes. Serve hot with butter and honey, if desired.

VARIATION

For savory biscuits, add ½ cup (60 g) shredded sharp cheddar cheese, 1½ tablespoons (5 g) minced fresh chives, and ¼ teaspoon freshly ground pepper to the flour and butter mixture before adding the buttermilk. You may need to use a little more buttermilk. The biscuits won't rise as high, but they will still be delicious.

Savory Cornbread with Jalapeños and Feta

To create the ultimate cornbread, our test kitchen filled it with colorful vegetables and feta. Jalapeños lend a spicy kick, and a mix of red and green ones will add an extra pop of color. Enjoy it alongside your favorite soup or chili or slather it with butter and honey for a decadent snack. Watch it closely as it bakes and cover the pan with foil if the toppings get too crisp.

MAKES 8 SERVINGS

CORNBREAD BATTER

1½ cups (210 g) medium-grind cornmeal

1 cup (140 g) all-purpose flour

2 teaspoons ground cumin

2 teaspoons baking powder

2 teaspoons kosher salt

½ teaspoon baking soda

½ teaspoon freshly ground pepper

1½ cups (360 g) sour cream

½ cup (120 g) unsalted butter, melted and cooled slightly

2 eggs

¼ cup (50 g) sugar

ADD-INS AND TOPPINGS

4 green onions, white and light green portions, thinly sliced on the diagonal

½ small red onion, minced

8 ounces (227 g) feta cheese, crumbled

1 ear of corn, shucked and kernels removed

2 jalapeños, 1 seeded and diced and 1 thinly sliced crosswise

Flaky sea salt

Extra-virgin olive oil, for drizzling

Preheat the oven to 350°F (180°C). Grease an 8½-by-4½-inch (21.5 by 11.5 cm) loaf pan with nonstick cooking spray.

To make the cornbread batter: In a medium bowl, whisk together the cornmeal, flour, cumin, baking powder, kosher salt, baking soda, and pepper. In a large bowl, whisk together the sour cream, melted butter, eggs, and sugar. Using a rubber spatula, fold in the cornmeal mixture until smooth.

To make the add-ins and toppings: Fold in all but 1 tablespoon each of the green onions, red onion, feta, and corn (reserve the rest for topping the batter), then fold in the diced jalapeño.

Transfer the batter to the prepared pan and smooth the top. Sprinkle with the reserved green onions, red onion, feta, and corn. Top with half of the sliced jalapeño and a generous sprinkling of flaky sea salt. Reserve the remaining jalapeño for garnishing the baked loaf.

Bake for 50 minutes. Remove the pan from the oven and drizzle the cornbread lightly with olive oil. Continue to bake until a toothpick inserted into the center comes out with only a few moist crumbs attached, 15 to 25 minutes more. If the toppings begin to get too crisp, cover the pan with aluminum foil.

Transfer the pan to a wire rack and let cool for 25 minutes. Carefully invert the loaf onto the rack and let cool for 5 minutes more. If some of the toppings fall off, carefully place them back on the loaf. Garnish with the remaining sliced jalapeño. Cut the cornbread into slices and serve warm or at room temperature.

Parker House Rolls

Parker House rolls are an American classic, and they're the perfect accompaniment for holiday feasts. Here, we've elevated them with a topping of flaky sea salt and a pat of honey butter for a sweet and salty take on this holiday favorite.

MAKES 24 ROLLS

ROLLS

1½ cups (360 ml) milk

½ cup (120 g) unsalted butter, cut into 8 pieces, plus 2 tablespoons (30 g) unsalted butter, melted

4½ teaspoons active dry yeast

3 tablespoons (36 g) plus 2 teaspoons sugar

4 cups (560 g) all-purpose flour, plus more for dusting

1 tablespoon (15 g) kosher salt

Vegetable oil, as needed

1½ teaspoons flaky sea salt

To make the rolls: In a small saucepan over medium heat, combine the milk and ½ cup (120 g) of butter. Heat until the butter is melted, about 7 minutes. Remove from the heat and let cool to 105° to 115°F (40° to 46°C). Add the yeast and 2 teaspoons of the sugar and stir until dissolved. Let stand for 10 minutes.

In the bowl of a stand mixer fitted with the dough hook, combine the flour, remaining 3 tablespoons (36 g) sugar, and kosher salt and beat on low speed until combined, about 30 seconds. Add the milk mixture and knead until the dough forms a ball, about 1 minute. Increase the speed to medium-low and knead until the dough is smooth and elastic, 4 to 5 minutes. Remove the dough from the mixer bowl, oil the inside of the bowl, and return the dough to the bowl. Cover tightly with plastic wrap and let the dough rise in a warm place until doubled in volume, about 1 hour. Divide the dough in half.

Grease a 9-by-13-inch (23 by 33 cm) baking pan. On a lightly floured work surface, roll each piece of dough into a log 12 inches (30.5 cm) long. Using a pastry scraper, divide each log into 12 equal pieces. Using the cupped palm of your hand, roll and shape each piece into a taut ball.

Transfer the dough balls to the prepared baking pan, arranging them so there are four rows of six. Cover tightly with plastic wrap and let rise in a warm place for 30 minutes.

HONEY BUTTER

½ cup (120 g) unsalted butter, at room temperature

1 heaping teaspoon honey

½ teaspoon kosher salt

Preheat the oven to 375°F (190°C).

Remove the plastic wrap from the pan. Brush the tops of the rolls with the 2 tablespoons (30 g) of melted butter and sprinkle with the flaky sea salt. Bake until the rolls are golden and an instant-read thermometer inserted into the center of a roll registers 190°F (88°C), 18 to 20 minutes.

Meanwhile, to make the honey butter: In a small bowl, stir together the butter, honey, and salt until thoroughly combined. Set aside at room temperature until ready to serve or refrigerate if you would prefer to serve the butter cold rather than softened.

Invert the rolls onto a wire rack, then turn them right side up onto another rack. Let cool slightly before serving with the honey butter alongside.

The Sweet Finale

Desserts for Every Occasion

Dessert is more than a sweet indulgence—it's a celebration, a comfort, and the perfect way to end any meal on a high note. In this chapter, you'll find recipes to match every mood and moment, from homey standards such as Classic Pound Cake (page 195) to showstopping favorites such as Crème Brûlée (page 221). Whether you're in the mood for something fruity and fresh, rich and chocolatey, or cool and creamy, these recipes are designed to deliver success and delight.

Triple Chocolate Layer Cake

This moist and tender chocolate cake is a showstopper, thanks to its added height from being baked in three 8-inch (20 cm) round cake pans. Topped with a simple, creamy chocolate ganache, it's easier to make than it looks. For an extra-indulgent dessert, serve each slice with a scoop of vanilla bean ice cream or a handful of fresh raspberries.

MAKES ONE 8-INCH (20 CM) THREE-LAYER CAKE, 12 SERVINGS

CAKE

2½ cups (350 g) all-purpose flour

2 cups (400 g) sugar

1 cup (90 g) unsweetened cocoa powder

1½ teaspoons baking powder

1½ teaspoons baking soda

½ teaspoon ground cinnamon

1½ teaspoons salt

3 eggs

1½ cups (360 ml) buttermilk

1 tablespoon (15 ml) pure vanilla extract

½ cup (120 ml) vegetable oil

1 cup (240 ml) boiling water

1 teaspoon espresso powder

To make the cake: Preheat the oven to 350°F (180°C). Grease three 8-inch (20 cm) round cake pans. Line the bottom of each pan with a round of parchment paper and grease the parchment.

In a mixing bowl, whisk together the flour, sugar, cocoa powder, baking powder, baking soda, cinnamon, and salt. Set aside. In the bowl of a stand mixer fitted with the whisk attachment, combine the eggs, buttermilk, vanilla, and vegetable oil. Beat on medium speed until thoroughly combined. Decrease the speed to low, slowly add the flour mixture, and mix until combined, stopping the mixer and scraping down the sides of the bowl as necessary.

In a small bowl, combine the boiling water and espresso powder and whisk until blended. With the mixer running on low speed, slowly add the espresso mixture to the batter. Stop the mixer and scrape down the sides of the bowl, then mix again until thoroughly combined, about 30 seconds.

Divide the batter evenly among the prepared cake pans. Smooth the tops with an offset spatula and tap the pans on the countertop to evenly distribute the batter. Bake until the cakes begin to pull away from the sides of the pan and a toothpick inserted into the center comes out clean, about 30 minutes. Transfer the pans to wire racks and let cool for 10 minutes, then turn the cakes out onto the racks and peel off the parchment paper. Let cool completely.

Continued on page 194

Continued from page 192

FROSTING

2 cups (360 g) semisweet chocolate chips

⅔ cup (160 ml) plus 2 tablespoons (30 ml) heavy cream

Cocoa powder, for dusting (optional)

Meanwhile, to make the frosting: Place the chocolate chips in a large heatproof mixing bowl. In a small saucepan over medium heat, warm the ⅔ cup (160 ml) of cream until simmering. Pour the hot cream over the chocolate chips and let stand for 5 minutes. Whisk the chocolate and cream until a smooth ganache forms. Let cool to room temperature. Transfer to the bowl of a stand mixer fitted with the whisk attachment and beat on high speed until the mixture begins to thicken. Add the remaining 2 tablespoons (30 ml) of cream and continue to beat on high speed until stiff peaks form, 3 to 4 minutes.

To assemble the cake, place one cake layer, top side up, on a cake stand or serving plate. Using an icing spatula, generously spread the cake layer with about a third of the frosting. Repeat the process with the remaining cake layers, spreading the remaining frosting on the last layer. Lightly dust the top of the cake with cocoa powder before cutting into slices and serving.

Classic Pound Cake

This rich, moist pound cake is incredibly versatile. Serve it on its own with seasonal fruit and ice cream or use it as a base for more elaborate desserts. It's perfect for an old-fashioned icebox cake, a trifle, or even split into layers for a cream-filled cake.

MAKES TWO 9-BY-5-INCH (23 BY 13 CM) LOAVES, 16 SERVINGS

- 1 cup (240 g) unsalted butter, at room temperature, plus more for pans and parchment paper
- 2 cups (180 g) all-purpose flour
- ½ teaspoon baking powder
- ¼ teaspoon salt
- 1½ cups (300 g) granulated sugar
- 4 eggs, lightly beaten
- 1 teaspoon pure vanilla extract
- ⅛ cup (60 ml) heavy cream
- Confectioners' sugar, for dusting

Preheat the oven to 325°F (170°C). Butter two 9-by-5-inch (23 by 13 cm) loaf pans and line them with buttered parchment paper.

In a bowl, sift together the flour, baking powder, and salt.

In a large bowl, using an electric mixer, beat together the butter and granulated sugar on medium speed until fluffy and lightened in color, about 2 minutes. Add the beaten eggs in four additions, beating well after each addition. Beat in the vanilla.

Decrease the speed to low. Add half the flour mixture and beat until incorporated. Beat in the cream until blended. Add the remaining flour mixture and beat just until a smooth batter forms.

Divide the batter evenly between the prepared pans. Bake until the tops are golden and a toothpick inserted into the centers comes out clean, about 1 hour.

Transfer the pans to a wire rack and let cool for about 20 minutes. Remove the cakes from the pans and let cool completely. Dust the tops of the cakes with confectioners' sugar and slice to serve.

Banana Bread with Chocolate Chips

Banana bread has that warm, comforting taste that makes every slice feel like home. For an extra touch, scatter chopped walnuts over the top before baking—the nuts toast as the loaf rises, adding a lovely crunch. And if you're a chocolate lover, turn it into a double-chocolate banana loaf by swapping in a bit of cocoa powder for some of the flour.

MAKES ONE 9-BY-5-INCH (23 BY 13 CM) LOAF, 6 TO 8 SERVINGS

½ cup (120 g) unsalted butter, at room temperature, plus more for greasing

1¾ cups (245 g) all-purpose flour, plus more for dusting

1 teaspoon baking soda

½ teaspoon baking powder

¼ teaspoon kosher salt

1 cup (200 g) sugar

2 large eggs, at room temperature

1 teaspoon pure vanilla extract

3 very ripe bananas, mashed (12 ounces [360 g])

½ cup (90 g) semisweet chocolate chips, plus more for sprinkling

Preheat the oven to 350°F (180°C). Butter and lightly flour a 9-by-5-inch (23 by 13 cm) loaf pan or three 3½-by-6-inch (9 by 15 cm) loaf pans.

In a bowl, sift together the flour, baking soda, baking powder, and salt. Set aside.

In the bowl of a stand mixer fitted with the paddle attachment, beat together the butter and sugar on medium speed until light and fluffy, about 3 minutes. Add the eggs one at a time, beating until incorporated after each addition, then add the vanilla and beat until smooth, about 1 minute. Decrease the speed to low, add the bananas, and beat until combined, about 30 seconds. Stop the mixer and scrape down the sides of the bowl. Add the flour mixture and beat on low speed just until the flour disappears, about 1 minute. Remove the bowl from the mixer. Using a rubber spatula, gently fold in the chocolate chips until evenly distributed. Pour the batter into the prepared pan(s) and spread evenly. Sprinkle with chocolate chips.

Bake until the bread is golden brown and a toothpick inserted into the center comes out clean, about 55 minutes for the large loaf and about 35 minutes for the small loaves.

Transfer the pan(s) to a wire rack and let cool for 15 minutes, then turn the bread out onto the rack and let cool completely. Cut into slices and serve.

Olive Oil Cake with Seasonal Fruit

This exceptionally moist and tender cake is filled with a trio of fresh berries, making it a welcome sight at any warm-weather gathering. It's a breeze to prepare—just whisk the ingredients together, fold in the fruit, and bake. Finish with a dusting of confectioners' sugar and a fresh fruit garnish for the perfect finishing touch.

MAKES ONE 9-INCH (23 CM) CAKE, 8 SERVINGS

2 cups (280 g) all-purpose flour, sifted

1 cup (200 g) granulated sugar

1 cup (225 g) firmly packed light brown sugar

1 teaspoon baking powder

1 teaspoon kosher salt

1 cup (240 ml) extra-virgin olive oil, plus more for greasing

1 cup (240 ml) milk

3 eggs

Grated zest of 1 lemon

½ cup (60 g) fresh blackberries, plus more for garnish

½ cup (60 g) fresh raspberries, plus more for garnish

½ cup (60 g) fresh blueberries, plus more for garnish

Confectioners' sugar, for dusting

1 nectarine, peeled, pitted, and sliced (optional)

Preheat the oven to 350°F (180°C). Grease a 9-inch (23 cm) round cake pan, line the bottom of the pan with parchment paper, then grease the parchment.

In a medium bowl, whisk together the flour, both sugars, baking powder, and salt. In a large bowl, whisk together the olive oil, milk, eggs, and lemon zest, then whisk in the flour mixture until combined. Using a rubber spatula, fold in the berries.

Pour the batter into the prepared pan. Bake until a toothpick inserted into the center of the cake comes out clean, about 1 hour. Transfer the pan to a wire rack and let cool for 10 minutes, then invert the cake onto the rack and let cool completely.

Just before serving, dust the cake with confectioners' sugar and garnish with berries and the nectarine slices, if using.

Carrot Cake with Cream Cheese Frosting

This moist carrot cake is a celebration of flavor. The mildly sweet taste from grated carrots and warm spices like cinnamon and ginger is perfectly complemented by a rich cream cheese frosting. The whimsical carrot tops "planted" in the frosting add a charming final touch, making the cake a perfect centerpiece for spring celebrations or any time of year.

MAKES ONE 9-INCH (23 CM) THREE-LAYER CAKE, 16 SERVINGS

CAKE

¾ cup (180 ml) canola oil, plus more for greasing

2¼ cups (315 g) all-purpose flour, plus more for dusting

2 teaspoons baking soda

2 teaspoons kosher salt

5 teaspoons ground cinnamon

2 teaspoons ground ginger

¼ teaspoon ground nutmeg

⅛ teaspoon ground cloves

3 large eggs

2¼ cups (450 g) granulated sugar

¾ cup (180 ml) buttermilk

2 teaspoons pure vanilla extract

6 ounces (180 g) canned crushed pineapple, drained

3 cups (330 g) grated peeled carrots

3 carrots, with tops attached

½ cup (60 g) chopped toasted walnuts

To make the cake: Preheat the oven to 350°F (180°C). Grease three 9-inch (23 cm) round cake pans, line the bottoms of the pans with parchment paper, then grease the parchment. Dust with flour, then tap out any excess.

In a large bowl, sift together the flour, baking soda, salt, cinnamon, ginger, nutmeg, and cloves. Set aside.

In the bowl of a stand mixer fitted with the paddle attachment, beat together the eggs, granulated sugar, oil, buttermilk, and vanilla on low speed until smooth, about 1 minute. Add the flour mixture in two additions and beat until combined, about 1 minute. Add the pineapple and grated carrots and beat until just incorporated.

Divide the batter evenly among the prepared pans and spread evenly. Bake until the tops of the cakes are browned and shiny and a toothpick inserted into the centers comes out clean, 25 to 30 minutes. Transfer the pans to wire racks and let cool for 10 minutes, then invert the cakes onto the racks and let cool completely.

Continued on page 202

Continued from page 200

FROSTING

1 cup (240 g) unsalted butter, at room temperature

3 cups (375 g) confectioners' sugar

½ teaspoon kosher salt

1 teaspoon pure vanilla extract

1 pound (450 g) cold cream cheese

2 tablespoons (30 g) heavy cream

To make the frosting: In the bowl of a stand mixer fitted with the paddle attachment, beat the butter on medium speed until smooth, about 1 minute. Decrease the speed to low, add the confectioners' sugar, and beat until combined, stopping the mixer to scrape down the sides of the bowl as needed. Add the salt and vanilla and increase the speed to medium-high. Add the cream cheese about 1 tablespoon (15 g) at a time and beat until combined and no bits of cream cheese remain, about 2 minutes. Increase the speed to high, add the cream, and beat until combined, 30 to 45 seconds.

To assemble the cake, place one cake layer on a cake stand or serving plate. Spread one-third of the cream cheese frosting evenly over the cake. Repeat with the remaining cake layers, including the top layer. Using an offset spatula, spread a thin layer of frosting on all sides of the cake to create a "naked" cake effect. Carefully peel the carrots, keeping the tops intact. Gently press the carrots into the top of the cake at varying heights. Scatter the walnuts around the carrots and serve.

Lemon Buttermilk Bars

These delightful dessert bars get their bright, tangy flavor from buttermilk, fresh lemon juice, and grated lemon zest. The result is a tender, moist bar with a perfect balance of sweet and tart. A simple dusting of confectioners' sugar adds an elegant finishing touch.

MAKES 8 BARS

6 tablespoons (90 g) unsalted butter, at room temperature, plus more for greasing

¼ cup (50 g) plus ⅔ cup (135 g) granulated sugar

⅔ cup (95 g) plus 2 tablespoons (16 g) all-purpose flour

⅛ teaspoon salt

2 eggs

1 tablespoon (6 g) finely grated lemon zest

⅓ cup (80 ml) fresh lemon juice

½ cup (120 ml) buttermilk

Confectioners' sugar, for dusting

Preheat the oven to 350°F (180°C). Butter the bottom and sides of an 8-inch (20 cm) square baking pan.

In a large bowl, using an electric mixer on medium speed, beat together the butter and the ¼ cup (50 g) of granulated sugar until creamy. Decrease the speed to low, add the ⅔ cup (95 g) of flour and the salt, and beat until blended. Spoon the dough into the prepared pan and press evenly into the pan bottom. Bake until the crust is golden, 15 to 18 minutes.

Meanwhile, in a large bowl, using an electric mixer on medium speed, beat the eggs and the remaining ⅔ cup (135 g) of granulated sugar until blended. Add the remaining 2 tablespoons (16 g) of flour, lemon zest, lemon juice, and buttermilk and beat until smooth. Pour the filling over the baked crust, spreading it evenly.

Bake until the top of the filling is set and barely browned at the edges, 20 to 25 minutes. Transfer the pan to a wire rack and let cool completely. Cut into 8 bars, dust with confectioners' sugar shaken through a sieve, and serve.

Perfect Chocolate Chip Cookies

For a taste of homemade comfort, bake a batch of our perfect chocolate chip cookies. With a soft, gooey center and a hint of caramel flavor, these cookies are studded with rich chocolate. For a foolproof way to get perfectly round cookies every time, our test kitchen recommends using a small ice cream scoop to portion the dough.

MAKES 10 TO 12 COOKIES

1¼ cups (175 g) unbleached all-purpose flour

1 teaspoon baking soda

½ teaspoon salt

½ cup (120 g) unsalted butter, at room temperature

½ cup (115 g) firmly packed light brown sugar

6 tablespoons (75 g) granulated sugar

1 egg

1 teaspoon pure vanilla extract

2½ cups (450 g) semisweet chocolate chips

In a bowl, sift together the flour, baking soda, and salt. In a large bowl, using an electric mixer on medium speed, beat the butter, brown sugar, and granulated sugar until smooth, about 2 minutes. Add the egg and vanilla and mix on low speed until blended. Slowly add the flour mixture and mix just until incorporated. Switch to a wooden spoon and stir in the chocolate chips.

Using a small ice cream scoop or heaping tablespoon, drop the dough onto the prepared baking sheets, spacing the dough mounds 2 inches (5 cm) apart.

Bake the cookies, one sheet at a time, until the bottoms and edges are lightly browned and the tops feel firm when lightly touched, 10 to 13 minutes. Let the cookies cool on the baking sheets for 5 minutes, then transfer the cookies to wire racks to cool completely.

Hazelnut and Dried Cherry Biscotti

Biscotti *means "twice baked" in Italian, and this double-baking process is the secret to their signature crunch. The dough is first baked in a loaf, then sliced and baked again until the cookies are golden and crisp. As durable as they are delicious, these cookies keep extremely well, making them a great choice for gift giving.*

MAKES 4 DOZEN BISCOTTI

½ cup (120 g) unsalted butter, at room temperature, plus more for greasing

¾ cup (150 g) granulated sugar

2 eggs

2 teaspoons pure vanilla extract

1¾ cups (245 g) all-purpose flour, plus more for dusting

½ teaspoon baking powder

½ teaspoon ground cinnamon

¼ teaspoon salt

1 cup (155 g) hazelnuts, toasted, skinned, and coarsely chopped

½ cup (90 g) dried tart cherries, coarsely chopped

1 teaspoon grated orange zest

Coarse sanding sugar, for sprinkling (optional)

Preheat the oven to 350°F (180°C). Lightly grease and flour a large baking sheet or line it with parchment paper. Have another ungreased baking sheet on hand.

In a large bowl, using an electric mixer on high speed, beat the butter until fluffy and pale yellow. Add the granulated sugar and continue beating until the mixture is no longer gritty when rubbed between your finger and thumb. Decrease the speed to low and add the eggs one at a time, beating well after each addition. Beat in the vanilla until blended.

Over a sheet of waxed paper, sift together the flour, baking powder, cinnamon, and salt. Gradually add the flour mixture to the egg mixture and beat on low speed or stir with a wooden spoon just until incorporated. Mix or stir in the hazelnuts, cherries, and orange zest until evenly distributed. The batter should be very soft.

Turn the batter out onto a generously floured work surface and divide in half. With well-floured hands, transfer one-half onto the greased baking sheet and shape into a log about 12 inches (30 cm) long and 1½ inches (4 cm) in diameter. Place on one side of the sheet. Repeat with the remaining batter, leaving at least 4 inches (10 cm) between the logs. (They will spread as they bake.)

Bake the logs until the edges are golden, 25 to 30 minutes. Transfer the pan to a wire rack and let the logs cool for 10 minutes. Sprinkle with sanding sugar, if desired. Using a serrated knife, cut the logs, still on the pan, on the diagonal into slices ½ inch (13 mm) thick. Carefully turn the slices on their sides and return them to the oven. When you run out of room on one baking sheet, start transferring slices to the other sheet.

Bake until the edges are golden, about 10 minutes more, turning the biscotti over halfway through the baking time. Let the biscotti cool completely on the pans on wire racks. Store in an airtight container.

Classic Cheesecake

The classic cheesecake is a timeless masterpiece, beloved for its velvety-smooth filling and rich, creamy texture. The luscious filling, made from cream cheese, eggs, and a touch of flavor, is baked to perfection inside a deep, golden crust of crushed graham crackers or cookies. Its simple elegance makes it the perfect canvas for a variety of toppings. Serve it with fresh berries, a drizzle of warm caramel, or a simple dollop of whipped cream. Remember to plan ahead, as the cheesecake needs to be refrigerated overnight to allow the filling to properly set.

MAKES ONE 9-INCH (23 CM) CAKE, 12 SERVINGS

CRUST

1¾ cups (175 g) graham cracker crumbs

¼ cup (55 g) firmly packed dark brown sugar

1 teaspoon grated lemon zest

½ cup (120 g) unsalted butter, melted and cooled

FILLING

2 pounds (900 g) cream cheese, at room temperature

1 cup (200 g) granulated sugar

1 cup (240 ml) heavy cream

1 teaspoon vanilla extract

1 tablespoon (15 ml) water

1 teaspoon unflavored gelatin

1½ cups (360 ml) cherry topping or 2 cups (300 g) fresh pitted cherries, for serving

To make the crust: Preheat the oven to 350°F (180°C).

In a food processor fitted with the metal blade, combine the graham cracker crumbs, brown sugar, and lemon zest and process to mix well. Add the butter and process until the crumbs begin to stick together. Drape your hand with plastic wrap to form a glove and press the crumbs evenly and firmly over the bottom and 2 inches (5 cm) up the side of a 9-by-2½-inch (23 by 6 cm) springform pan. Bake the crust for 10 minutes. Remove from the oven and cool to room temperature, about 30 minutes.

To make the filling: In a large bowl, combine the cream cheese and granulated sugar. Using an electric mixer, beat on medium speed until well blended. Beat in ½ cup (120 ml) of the cream and the vanilla until incorporated.

Place the water in a small saucepan. Sprinkle the gelatin over the water and let soften for 5 minutes. Place the saucepan over low heat and stir until the gelatin is dissolved, then gradually whisk in the remaining ½ cup (120 ml) of cream. Add the gelatin mixture to the cream cheese mixture and beat until fluffy, about 1 minute. Spoon the filling into the cooled crust. Cover with aluminum foil and refrigerate overnight or up to 2 days.

To serve, run a knife around the pan sides to loosen the cake. Release the pan sides and place the cake on a plate. Cut the cake into individual slices and spoon cherries over each slice.

Chocolate Crinkle Cookies

These cookies are a dream for any chocolate lover. With a crisp, crackled exterior and a chewy, fudgy interior, they deliver a rich and decadent chocolate flavor that satisfies the most serious cravings. A dusting of confectioners' sugar before baking gives them their distinctive look, making them as elegant as they are delicious.

MAKES ABOUT 24 COOKIES

½ cup (120 g) unsalted butter, at room temperature, plus more for greasing

½ cup (60 g) confectioners' sugar

1⅔ cups (235 g) all-purpose flour

½ cup (45 g) unsweetened cocoa powder

1½ teaspoons baking powder

¼ teaspoon salt

1¼ cups (250 g) granulated sugar

2 eggs

½ teaspoon pure vanilla extract

Preheat the oven to 350°F (180°C). Grease two baking sheets with butter. Put the confectioners' sugar into a bowl and set aside.

In another bowl, using a wooden spoon, stir together the flour, cocoa powder, baking powder, and salt. Set aside.

In a large bowl, using an electric mixer on medium speed, beat the butter and granulated sugar until creamy, about 3 minutes. Turn off the mixer and scrape down the bowl with a rubber spatula. Add 1 egg and beat on medium speed until blended. Add the other egg and vanilla and beat until blended.

Turn off the mixer and add the flour mixture. Beat on low speed just until blended.

Using a tablespoon, scoop up a rounded spoonful of dough. Using your hands, roll the dough into a ball, then roll the ball in the confectioners' sugar until covered. Place the ball on one of the prepared baking sheets. Repeat, spacing the balls about 2 inches (5 cm) apart.

When one baking sheet is full, put it in the oven and bake the cookies until they are crackled and puffed, 10 to 12 minutes. Transfer the cookies to a wire rack and let cool completely. Repeat to bake the remaining cookies.

Chuck's Madeleines

With their elegant, shell-shaped design, these fragrant, cakelike cookies are a joy to bake. Flavored with delicate orange flower water, they are a nod to the past—madeleine pans were among the first baking tools Chuck Williams brought to America in the late 1950s. For a perfect, light texture, our test kitchen recommends sifting the flour before measuring.

MAKES 12 MADELEINES

4 tablespoons (60 g) unsalted butter, at room temperature, plus more for greasing

½ cup (60 g) cake flour

½ teaspoon baking powder

1 egg

¼ cup (50 g) granulated sugar

2 teaspoons orange flower water

Confectioners' sugar, for dusting

CHUCK'S TIP

These little sponge cakes, immortalized by Marcel Proust in Remembrance of Things Past, are at their most memorable when eaten as Proust himself liked them—fresh from the oven, still warm, and a little crisp on the outside.

Position a rack in the lower third of the oven and preheat to 400°F (200°C). Generously butter a 12-mold madeleine pan.

In a bowl, sift together the flour and baking powder. In another bowl, using an electric mixer on medium speed, beat together the egg, granulated sugar, and orange flower water for 30 seconds. Increase the speed to high and beat until the mixture has quadrupled in bulk and is very thick, about 10 minutes. Using a rubber spatula, carefully fold the flour mixture and then the softened butter into the egg mixture. Spoon the batter into the prepared molds, filling each one about three-fourths full.

Bake until the madeleines are lightly browned around the edges and on the bottom, 10 to 12 minutes. Remove the madeleines from the oven and immediately turn them out onto a wire rack. Using a fine-mesh sieve or a sifter, dust them with confectioners' sugar. Serve warm.

NOTE

Madeleine pans typically have 8 or 12 shallow molds and come in tinned steel, metal with a nonstick finish, or pliable silicone. If you use a black nonstick madeleine pan, decrease the oven temperature to 375°F (190°C) or shorten the baking time by a few minutes.

Flourless Chocolate Torte

For best results, always use a spotlessly clean bowl and beater, as any trace of grease or egg yolk will prevent the whites from expanding to their full volume. Take care not to overbeat, or they will become clumpy and grainy. Finally, gently fold the beaten whites into the batter to prevent them from deflating. Remember to plan ahead, as the torte needs to be refrigerated for at least 4 hours after baking to properly set.

MAKES 14 SERVINGS

1 cup plus 2 tablespoons (270 g) unsalted butter, cut into small pieces, plus more for greasing

Unsweetened cocoa powder, for dusting

15 ounces (450 g) bittersweet chocolate, finely chopped

7 egg yolks

9 tablespoons (110 g) granulated sugar

1½ tablespoons (23 ml) dark rum or brewed espresso (optional)

1½ teaspoons pure vanilla extract

Pinch of salt

5 egg whites, at room temperature

3 cups (360 g) raspberries

Confectioners' sugar, for dusting

Preheat the oven to 300°F (150°C). Grease a heart-shaped springform cake pan with butter and dust with cocoa powder.

In the top pan of a double boiler, combine the butter and chocolate. Set the top pan over but not touching barely simmering water in the bottom pan and melt, then whisk until well blended. Set aside to cool slightly.

In a large bowl, using an electric mixer fitted with the whisk attachment on medium-high speed, beat together the egg yolks, 6 tablespoons (75 g) of the granulated sugar, rum, vanilla, and salt until pale and very thick, 3 to 5 minutes. Gradually pour in the chocolate mixture and continue beating until well blended.

In a deep, clean bowl, using a mixer fitted with a clean whisk attachment, beat the egg whites on medium-high speed until foamy, about 1 minute. Gradually add the remaining 3 tablespoons (35 g) of granulated sugar and continue to beat until medium-firm peaks form, about 2 minutes. Scoop half of the egg whites onto the chocolate mixture and fold them in gently. Fold in the remaining whites just until no streaks remain.

Pour the batter into the prepared pan and spread it out evenly. Bake until the torte puffs slightly and a toothpick inserted into the center comes out very moist but not liquid, about 40 minutes. Do not overcook. Transfer the pan to a wire rack and let cool for 30 minutes.

To remove the pan sides, set the pan on a can and let the sides slide down. Let the torte cool completely, then cover and refrigerate until very cold, at least 4 hours or up to overnight.

Just before serving, garnish the torte with the raspberries and dust with confectioners' sugar.

Apple Galette

This beautiful, free-form tart will impress your guests at any autumn gathering. A mandoline makes fast work of cutting the apples into uniform, thin slices, and there's no need to peel the apples first, as the red color peeking through is part of the dessert's rustic appeal.

MAKES 8 SERVINGS

FILLING

3 medium red apples, cored, quartered, and thinly sliced into crescent moons on a mandoline

1 tablespoon (12 g) cane sugar

Juice of ½ lemon

Small pinch of kosher salt

CRUST

1¼ cups (175 g) unbleached all-purpose flour, plus more for dusting

1 tablespoon (12 g) granulated sugar

¼ teaspoon kosher salt

½ cup (120 g) cold unsalted butter, cut into ¼-inch (6 mm) cubes

3 tablespoons (45 ml) very cold water

1 egg whisked with 1 teaspoon water

Turbinado sugar, for sprinkling

Apricot jam, for brushing

Vanilla ice cream, for serving

Preheat the oven to 350°F (180°C). Line a baking sheet with parchment paper.

To make the filling: In a bowl, gently toss together the apple slices, cane sugar, and lemon juice until combined. Add the salt and toss again. Set aside.

To make the crust: In the bowl of an electric mixer fitted with the flat beater, stir together the flour, granulated sugar, and salt. Add the butter and toss with a fork to coat with the flour mixture. Beat on medium-low speed until the texture resembles coarse cornmeal, with the butter pieces no larger than small peas. Add the water and beat on low speed just until the dough pulls together.

Transfer the dough to a work surface, pat into a ball, and flatten into a disk. (Although many dough recipes call for chilling the dough at this point, this dough should be rolled out immediately for the best results.)

Lightly flour the work surface, then flatten the disk with six to eight gentle taps of the rolling pin. Lift the dough and give it a quarter turn. Lightly dust the top of the dough or the rolling pin with flour as needed, then roll out into a round at least 12 inches (30 cm) in diameter and about ⅛ inch (3 mm) thick. Using a pizza cutter, trim the dough to create a smooth edge. Transfer the dough to the prepared baking sheet.

Arrange the apple slices in the center of the dough, overlapping them at the edges and spiraling them inward or arranging in another design, leaving a 2-inch (5 cm) border uncovered. Gently fold the edges of the dough over itself, forming loose pleats. Brush the pleated dough with the egg wash and sprinkle lightly with turbinado sugar.

Bake until the crust is golden and the apples are just tender, about 25 minutes.

Transfer the baking sheet to a wire rack and lightly brush the apricot jam over the apples. Serve warm or let the galette cool completely. Cut into slices and serve with vanilla ice cream.

Key Lime Pie

For a delightful twist, this Key lime pie recipe swaps the traditional graham cracker crust for one made of sweet and spicy gingersnaps. The bold flavor of the cookies provides a perfect contrast to the pie's tangy lime filling. Remember to plan ahead, as the pie needs to be refrigerated for several hours after baking to allow the filling to properly set.

MAKES ONE 9-INCH (23 CM) PIE, 8 SERVINGS

CRUST

10 ounces (300 g) gingersnaps

5 tablespoons (75 g) unsalted butter, melted

2 tablespoons (25 g) granulated sugar

½ teaspoon salt

FILLING

2 egg yolks

One 14-ounce (420 g) can sweetened condensed milk

2 teaspoons grated Key lime zest

½ cup (120 ml) Key lime juice

WHIPPED CREAM

2 cups (480 ml) heavy cream

1 teaspoon pure vanilla extract

¼ cup (50 g) superfine sugar

Preheat the oven to 350°F (180°C).

To make the crust: In a food processor, process the gingersnaps until fine crumbs form. Add the melted butter, granulated sugar, and salt and pulse until moistened. Press the mixture firmly into the bottom and up the sides of a 9-inch (23 cm) pie dish. Place on a baking sheet and bake until the edges are dry and set, 5 to 7 minutes. The bottom will still be moist and soft but will firm up as the crust cools. Transfer to a wire rack and let cool completely. Keep the oven set at 350°F (180°C).

To make the filling: In a bowl, using an electric mixer on medium speed, beat the egg yolks until blended. Add the condensed milk, lime zest, and lime juice and continue beating until well blended. Pour the filling into the cooled crust and bake until the edges of the pie are set but the center still jiggles slightly, 15 to 20 minutes. Transfer the pie to a wire rack and let cool completely. Refrigerate the pie for at least 2 hours or up to overnight to allow it to set.

When ready to serve the pie, make the whipped cream: In the bowl of an electric mixer fitted with the whisk attachment, combine the cream and vanilla. With the mixer set on low speed, slowly add the superfine sugar while beating, gradually increasing the speed as the mixture thickens. Continue to beat until soft peaks form, about 2 minutes total.

To serve the pie, cut into 8 slices and garnish each slice with a heaping spoonful of the whipped cream.

Blackberry Crumble

The apples in this crumble will remain a bit firm after baking. If you prefer a softer texture, microwave them for 7 minutes before mixing with the berries. You can also make the crumble mixture in bulk to have on hand for quick desserts. It keeps for up to 4 weeks in the refrigerator or can be frozen for longer storage.

MAKES 8 SERVINGS

4 apples (such as Granny Smith, Honeycrisp, or Pink Lady)

4 cups (600 g) fresh or frozen blackberries or blueberries

2 teaspoons cornstarch

½ cup (100 g) granulated sugar

¾ cup (105 g) all-purpose flour

¾ cup (165 g) firmly packed brown sugar

1 cup (80 g) old-fashioned rolled oats

½ cup (40 g) shredded dried coconut

½ cup (60 g) chopped almonds

2 teaspoons ground cinnamon

½ teaspoon ground ginger

½ cup (120 g) unsalted butter, melted

Preheat the oven to 325°F (170°C).

Peel, core, and thinly slice the apples.

In a bowl, stir together the apples, berries, cornstarch, and granulated sugar. Spread the fruit mixture in a baking dish that is 12 to 14 inches (30.5 to 35.5 cm) in diameter.

In a bowl, stir together the flour, brown sugar, oats, coconut, almonds, cinnamon, and ginger. Drizzle with the melted butter and toss with a fork to combine. Sprinkle the crumble mixture evenly over the fruit. Bake until golden and crisp, 45 to 50 minutes. Serve warm.

Tiramisù

There are few desserts quite as elegant and timeless as tiramisù. With its layers of rum-and-espresso-soaked ladyfingers and a rich mascarpone cream, this classic Italian dessert is a celebration of flavor and texture. It's the perfect finale for a dinner party, and best of all, you can make it a day ahead for easy entertaining. Remember to plan ahead, as the tiramisù needs to be refrigerated for at least 4 hours to properly set.

MAKES 12 SERVINGS

- 6 egg yolks
- ¾ cup (150 g) sugar
- 1 pound (450 g) mascarpone cheese, softened
- 2 cups (480 ml) chilled heavy cream
- 2 tablespoons (30 ml) rum
- 1 teaspoon pure vanilla extract
- 2 tablespoons (30 ml) plus 2 to 3 cups (480 to 720 ml) brewed espresso
- 5 egg whites
- 40 to 50 ladyfingers
- Cocoa powder, for dusting

In a mixing bowl set over a pan of simmering water but not touching the water, whisk the egg yolks and sugar until the mixture is pale yellow and thick ribbons fall from the whisk, 4 to 5 minutes. Transfer the mixture to the bowl of an electric mixer. Add the mascarpone cheese and beat until smooth and creamy, 2 to 3 minutes.

In a chilled large mixing bowl, whisk the cream until stiff peaks form. Add the rum, vanilla, and the 2 tablespoons (30 ml) of espresso and whisk until smooth.

In a clean mixing bowl, whisk the egg whites until stiff peaks form. (When the whisk is lifted straight out of the bowl and inverted, the whites should hold their shape.)

With a rubber spatula, gently fold the mascarpone mixture into the cream until blended and smooth. Add about one-third of the egg whites and fold gently until blended. Add the remaining egg whites and fold gently until the mixture is smooth and blended.

One at a time, submerge the ladyfingers into the remaining 2 to 3 cups (480 to 720 ml) of espresso. Lay enough ladyfingers on the bottom of a 6-quart (5.4 L) glass or ceramic baking or serving dish (about 2 inches [5 cm] deep) to form a single layer. Spread half of the mascarpone mixture over the ladyfingers until evenly covered. Arrange another layer of ladyfingers over the mascarpone cream, then spread the remaining mascarpone cream evenly over the top. Dust the tiramisù with cocoa powder to create a rich, dark topping. Refrigerate for at least 4 hours or up to 1 day before serving.

Crème Brûlée

With its rich, velvety custard and crackling sugar crust, this crème brûlée is always a crowd-pleaser. For easy entertaining, the custards can be baked up to 3 days in advance. All that's left to do is sprinkle them with a little sugar and caramelize the tops. Remember to plan ahead, as the crème brûlée needs to be refrigerated for at least 2 hours after baking to allow the filling to properly set.

MAKES 8 SERVINGS

8 egg yolks

⅓ cup (65 g) plus 8 teaspoons sugar

2 cups (480 ml) heavy cream

1 teaspoon vanilla bean paste

Pinch of kosher salt

Fresh berries, for serving (optional)

In a large bowl, whisk together the egg yolks and the ⅓ cup (65 g) of sugar until the sugar has dissolved and the mixture is thick and pale yellow, about 5 minutes. Add the cream, vanilla, and salt and whisk until well blended. Strain the mixture into a large liquid measuring cup or a pitcher, skimming off any foam or bubbles.

Fill a pitcher with enough water to fill the air cooker tray of a Philips Airfryer. Set aside.

Divide the egg mixture among eight 3-ounce (90 g) ramekins. Using a spoon, gently skim off any visible foam or bubbles. Carefully place 4 ramekins in the air fryer tray.

Fill the tray with enough water from the pitcher to come about two-thirds up the sides of the ramekins. Set the air fryer to 300°F (150°C). Bake until the custards are set around the edges but are still loose in the center, 15 to 20 minutes.

Remove the tray from the air fryer and let the ramekins stand in the water bath until cool, then remove them from the water bath. Pour out the water in the tray. Repeat to cook the remaining 4 ramekins, using fresh water in the tray, then let the custards cool. Cover the ramekins with plastic wrap and refrigerate for at least 2 hours or up to 2 days.

When ready to serve, sprinkle 1 teaspoon of sugar over each custard. For best results, use a kitchen torch to melt the sugar according to the manufacturer's instructions. Alternatively, heat a broiler on the highest setting, then place the ramekins on the top rack 4 to 6 inches (10 to 15 cm) from the heat source; broil until the sugar melts and caramelizes, 3 to 5 minutes. Refrigerate the custards for a few minutes before serving to set the crème brûlée. Serve with fresh berries, if desired.

Chocolate Pudding Pie

To make decorative chocolate curls, warm a medium-size chunk of semisweet chocolate by rubbing it between your hands for 1 or 2 minutes. For larger pieces, microwave on low for about 5 seconds. Once the chocolate is warmed but not melted, unwrap it and use a vegetable peeler to slowly and evenly scrape the edge. Repeat the warming process as needed to create more curls. Remember to plan ahead, as the pie needs to be refrigerated for 2 to 3 hours to allow the filling to properly set.

MAKES ONE 9-INCH (23 CM) PIE, 8 SERVINGS

FILLING

2½ cups (600 ml) milk

5 ounces (150 g) semisweet chocolate, chopped into slivers

4 egg yolks

¾ cup (150 g) sugar

3 tablespoons (30 g) cornstarch

¼ teaspoon salt

1½ teaspoons pure vanilla extract

1 Cookie Crumb Crust (page 223), made with chocolate cookies

TOPPING

1 cup (240 ml) heavy cream

1 tablespoon (12 g) sugar

1 teaspoon pure vanilla extract

Chocolate curls, for decorating (see headnote)

To make the filling: In a heavy nonaluminum saucepan over low heat, warm the milk and chocolate, whisking until the chocolate is melted; the mixture will be speckled.

In a bowl, whisk together the egg yolks and sugar until pale yellow. Add the cornstarch and salt, then the vanilla, and whisk until well blended. Slowly pour the warm chocolate mixture into the yolk mixture, whisking constantly until well blended. Return the mixture to the saucepan and cook over medium heat until it thickens and begins to bubble slowly, 6 to 8 minutes. Remove from the heat and stir until smooth, about 1 minute.

Pour the filling into the crumb crust and smooth with a spatula. Cover with plastic wrap, pressing it directly onto the surface, and refrigerate until completely cold and firm, 2 to 3 hours.

Just before serving, make the topping: Using an electric mixer on medium-high speed or a whisk, beat together the cream, sugar, and vanilla until stiff peaks form. Spread the whipped cream on top of the pie. Decorate with chocolate curls. Refrigerate until ready to serve but let the pie stand at room temperature for 20 minutes before serving to take the chill off.

Cookie Crumb Crust

Quick and easy to assemble, with no rolling required, this crust forms the base for simple pies, such as Chocolate Pudding Pie (page 222) and Mississippi mud pie. It's a great go-to crust for when you're short on time but still want a delicious homemade dessert.

MAKES ONE 9-INCH (23 CM) CRUST

- 1¼ cups (125 g) cookie crumbs, such as graham crackers, chocolate wafers, or gingersnaps
- 5 tablespoons (75 g) unsalted butter, melted
- 3 tablespoons (35 g) sugar

Preheat the oven to 350°F (180°C).

In a bowl, combine the cookie crumbs, butter, and sugar and stir until the crumbs are well moistened. Pat the mixture firmly and evenly into the bottom and all the way up the sides of a 9-inch (23 cm) pie pan or dish.

Bake until the crust is firm, about 5 minutes. For a firmer, crunchier crust, bake for 5 minutes more.

Blueberry Pavlova Cake

This showstopping pavlova is a perfect centerpiece for summer gatherings. Our test kitchen transforms airy meringue into blossom shapes, then layers them with whipped cream, a sweet blueberry compote, and fresh berries. For easy entertaining, you can prepare the compote and bake the meringues ahead of time. The compote works beautifully with either fresh or frozen blueberries. Remember to plan ahead, as the pavlovas need to cool in the oven for at least 2 hours to allow them to properly set.

MAKES 6 SERVINGS

PAVLOVAS

8 egg whites, at room temperature

2 tablespoons (20 g) cornstarch, sifted

2 cups (400 g) granulated sugar

4 teaspoons pure vanilla extract

To make the pavlovas: Position a rack in the lower third of the oven and preheat to 250°F (120°C). Draw three 6-inch (15 cm) flower or blossom shapes on a sheet of parchment paper. Turn the parchment over and place on a baking sheet.

In the bowl of an electric mixer fitted with the whisk attachment, beat the egg whites on medium speed until well combined, about 1 minute. Sprinkle the cornstarch over the egg whites and beat until foamy, about 3 minutes. Increase the speed to high and very gradually add the granulated sugar, beating until stiff, shiny peaks form, 8 to 10 minutes. Quickly beat in the vanilla.

Transfer the meringue to a large piping bag fitted with a ¼- to ½-inch (6 to 13 mm) open tip. Pipe a small amount of the meringue under each of the four corners of the parchment paper, then press down to adhere. This will stabilize the parchment on the baking sheet, facilitating the piping process.

Pipe equal amounts of the meringue onto the flower or blossom shapes on the parchment, filling them in completely. Use the back of a spoon to create an indentation in the center of each meringue. Pipe some smaller stars and dollops on the parchment to use for decoration.

Bake until the meringues are crisp and the color has deepened slightly, about 1 hour. Turn off the oven and, leaving the door closed, let the meringues cool in the oven for at least 2 hours or up to overnight.

Continued on page 226

Continued from page 224

BLUEBERRY COMPOTE

2 pounds (940 g) small fresh blueberries or frozen blueberries

½ cup (100 g) granulated sugar

¾ cup (180 ml) water, plus more as needed

6 tablespoons (90 ml) fresh orange juice

FOR SERVING

2 cups (480 ml) cold heavy cream, whipped to soft peaks

Fresh blueberries, for garnish

Fresh blackberries, for garnish

Freeze-dried blueberries, for garnish (optional)

Confectioners' sugar, for dusting

To make the blueberry compote: In a saucepan over medium heat, combine the blueberries, granulated sugar, water, and orange juice and bring to a vigorous simmer. Cook, stirring occasionally, for 6 to 8 minutes; the berries will release their juices and then begin to absorb them as the compote thickens. Remove from the heat and let cool completely. The compote will thicken as it cools. (If you want a thicker compote, cook for 2 minutes more before cooling; for a thinner one, stir 1 tablespoon [15 ml] of water into the cooled compote.) The compote can be refrigerated in an airtight container for up to 1 week.

To serve: Place one of the pavlovas on a cake stand or a serving platter. Dollop a generous amount of whipped cream into the hollow of the meringue, then top with about one-third each of the compote, fresh blueberries, and blackberries. Top with a second pavlova, dollop with whipped cream, and top with about half of the remaining compote and berries. Repeat the process with the third pavlova and the remaining whipped cream, compote, and berries. Arrange the smaller meringues around the top layer for decoration. Using a microplane, carefully grate freeze-dried blueberries over the top, if desired. Dust with confectioners' sugar and serve immediately.

Vanilla Bean Panna Cotta

Panna cotta, which means "cooked cream" in Italian, is a specialty of Italy's Piedmont region. This elegant dessert has the pure flavor of fresh cream and a smooth, custard-like consistency thanks to a touch of gelatin. For a delicate aroma, use a vanilla bean. Alternatively, 1 teaspoon of vanilla extract can be substituted; just add it after you remove the pan from the heat. Remember to plan ahead, as the panna cottas need to be refrigerated for at least 4 hours to allow them to properly set.

MAKES 4 SERVINGS

One 2½-teaspoon (7 g) package unflavored gelatin

¼ cup (60 ml) milk

2 cups (480 ml) heavy cream

¼ cup (50 g) sugar

1 vanilla bean

4 cups (600 g) berries, such as blackberries, sliced strawberries, blueberries, and/or raspberries, in any combination

In a large bowl, sprinkle the gelatin over the milk. Let stand for about 2 minutes to soften the gelatin.

In a saucepan over medium heat, stir together the cream and sugar. Using a small, sharp knife, split the vanilla bean in half lengthwise. Using the tip of the knife, scrape the seeds from the vanilla bean into the cream. Add the vanilla bean pod to the cream. Heat, stirring occasionally, until small bubbles appear around the edges of the pan. Remove from the heat and let cool briefly.

Remove the vanilla bean pod. Slowly add the warm cream to the gelatin mixture, stirring constantly until completely dissolved. Pour the mixture into four ¾-cup (180 g) ramekins or custard cups, dividing it evenly. Cover and refrigerate for at least 4 hours or up to overnight.

When ready to serve, run a small knife blade around the inside of each ramekin to loosen the panna cotta, then invert each ramekin onto a dessert plate. Arrange the berries around the panna cotta and serve immediately.

Fresh Strawberry Ice Cream

For the most intensely sweet aroma and flavor, make this ice cream at the peak of strawberry season, from April to June. If you can find wild strawberries, also known as fraises des bois, this variety will produce an unparalleled flavor. The result is a silky-smooth, vibrant pink ice cream that tastes like pure summer.

MAKES 1 QUART (940 G), 6 SERVINGS

3 cups (720 ml) half-and-half

6 egg yolks

1 cup (200 g) sugar

Pinch of salt

2 cups (340 g) sliced strawberries

1 teaspoon pure vanilla extract

In a saucepan over medium heat, warm the half-and-half until steam begins to rise from the surface, 4 to 5 minutes.

In a heatproof bowl, whisk together the egg yolks, sugar, and salt until blended. Gradually add the hot half-and-half, whisking constantly until fully incorporated. Transfer the mixture to a clean saucepan and set over medium-low heat. Cook, stirring constantly with a wooden spoon or spatula, until the custard is thick enough to coat the back of the spoon and leaves a clear trail when a finger is drawn through it, 8 to 10 minutes; do not allow the custard to boil.

Pour the custard through a fine-mesh sieve set over a clean bowl and stir in the strawberries and vanilla. Nestle the bowl in a larger one filled halfway with ice and water and cool the custard to room temperature, stirring occasionally. Refrigerate until cold, at least 1 hour.

Transfer the custard to an ice cream maker and freeze according to the manufacturer's instructions. Transfer the ice cream to a freezer-safe container. Cover and freeze until firm, at least 3 hours or up to 3 days, before serving.

Chocolate Pots de Crème

The sign of a well-made pot de crème is texture: every spoonful of the custard should be creamy and rich. To protect custards from overheating and curdling, they are traditionally baked in a water bath. This recipe, however, uses a steam oven to provide the same gentle heat, making the process effortless and eliminating the need for a water bath. Remember to plan ahead, as the pots de crème need to be refrigerated for at least 4 hours to allow them to properly set.

MAKES 4 SERVINGS

2 ounces (60 g) bittersweet chocolate, chopped into small pieces

1 cup (240 ml) heavy cream

3 egg yolks

2 tablespoons (25 g) sugar

1 teaspoon vanilla extract

¼ teaspoon salt

Put the chocolate in a heatproof bowl. In a saucepan over medium heat, warm the cream until small bubbles appear around the edges. Remove from the heat and pour over the chocolate. Let stand for 5 minutes, then stir until the chocolate is completely melted.

In a bowl, whisk together the egg yolks and sugar until pale yellow, about 3 minutes. Add a spoonful of the chocolate cream and whisk until fully incorporated. Slowly stir in the remaining chocolate cream, then stir in the vanilla and salt.

Place four 5-ounce (150 g) ramekins on the baking tray of a Cuisinart steam oven. Strain the chocolate mixture through a fine-mesh sieve into a large heatproof liquid measuring cup, then pour into the ramekins, dividing it evenly. Cover the ramekins with aluminum foil.

Position a rack in the lower rung of the steam oven. Transfer the tray to the oven. Turn the oven to the bake/steam setting at 170°F (77°C) according to the manufacturer's instructions. Bake for 40 minutes. Remove the foil and turn the oven to bake/steam at 180°F (82°C). Bake for 20 minutes more, or until the custard has set around the edges but is still soft in the center.

CHUCK'S TIP

Before our obsession with chocolate mousse, lovers of French cooking were filling individual porcelain pots with rich, dense chocolate custard. Although this dessert looks sophisticated, there is no great secret to success. Just start with the right kind of small, heatproof cups and a good-quality French, Swiss, or Belgian bittersweet chocolate such as Callebaut, Valrhona, Tobler, or Lindt.

Alternative Method

If you don't have a steam oven, bake the custards in a traditional water bath. Arrange the filled ramekins in a deep baking dish and pour in enough hot water to reach halfway up their sides. Bake in a conventional oven at 300°F (150°C) for about 45 to 50 minutes, or until the custards are set around the edges but still slightly jiggly in the center.

Transfer the ramekins to a wire rack and let cool to room temperature. Cover with plastic wrap and refrigerate for at least 4 hours or up to 2 days before serving.

The Art of Entertaining

Menus and Tips for Special Moments

Whether it's a carefree brunch with friends, a dinner outdoors, or an elegant evening celebration, every occasion deserves food and drink that feel special. These menus are designed for memorable moments, from bubbly cocktails and small bites to stunning mains and showstopping desserts. You'll find inspiration for every kind of gathering: a boozy brunch filled with bright flavors, a leisurely al fresco spread for warm evenings, a Parisian dream of timeless French classics, cozy holiday favorites for the season, and an elegant soirée with dishes made to impress. With these recipes, entertaining becomes effortless, inviting, and always delicious.

Boozy Brunch

Brunch is a beautiful thing. It's a chance to relax and enjoy a leisurely meal, especially when it's filled with savory dishes and a little something special to drink. This menu delivers on all counts, from the sparkling limoncello spritz to the savory bacon and leek quiche.

Limoncello Spritz (page 39)

Mini Crab Cakes with Lemon Aioli (page 44)

Bacon and Leek Quiche (page 71)

Prosciutto-Wrapped Asparagus (page 47)

Banana Bread with Chocolate Chips (page 197)

Dining Al Fresco

Dining outdoors is perfect for its ease and charm: fresh air, good company, and food that feels both relaxed and celebratory. This menu is designed to please a variety of tastes, from refreshing Spanish G&Ts and vibrant baked feta to grilled lobster, juicy chicken, and a sweet scoop of strawberry ice cream to finish.

Spanish G&T (page 29)

Baked Feta with Sumac Grapes and Green Olives (page 62)

Grilled Lobster with Lemon Butter (page 157)

Honey-Lime Grilled Chicken (page 158)

Fresh Strawberry Ice Cream (page 229)

Dreaming of Paris

Bring the romance of Paris to your table with this elegant menu. Sip a sparkling French 75, nibble on warm gougères, and savor classics like French onion soup and roast chicken with lemon. End the evening on a sweet note with the ultimate French finale: crème brûlée!

French 75 (page 28)

Gougères (page 64)

French Onion Soup (page 85)

Simple Roast Chicken with Lemon (page 90)

Crème Brûlée (page 221)

Home for the Holidays

The holidays call for comfort, tradition, and a touch of indulgence. This menu brings it all together starting with a cozy maple bourbon smash and a decadent baked Brie, followed by the timeless elegance of beef bourguignon with golden popovers. An apple galette, rustic yet refined, makes the perfect sweet ending to a festive feast shared with loved ones.

Maple Bourbon Smash (page 27)

Baked Brie en Croûte with Apple Compote (page 59)

Beef Bourguignon with Boiled Potatoes and Parsley (page 100)

Perfect Popovers (page 172)

Apple Galette (page 215)

An Elegant Soirée

Designed for evenings that call for sophistication, this menu combines luxurious flavors with effortless style. Sip on jewel-toned pomegranate Cosmopolitans while nibbling on caviar-topped phyllo cups and savory stuffed mushrooms. A tender beef roast, paired with creamy potato leek gratin and a vibrant market salad, sets the stage for a refined main course. And for the grand finale, a flourless chocolate torte delivers the perfect touch of decadence.

Pomegranate Cosmopolitan (page 35)

Phyllo Cups with Caviar and Crème Fraîche (page 51)

Stuffed Mushrooms (page 48)

Potato Leek Gratin (page 102)

Pan-Roasted Beef Tenderloin with Rosemary and Garlic (page 93)

Farmers' Market Salad with Whipped Ricotta (page 109)

Flourless Chocolate Torte (page 212)

Index

C

D

E

F

G

weldon**owen**
an imprint of Insight Editions
P.O. Box 3088
San Rafael, CA 94912
www.weldonowen.com

CEO Raoul Goff
SVP Group Publisher Jeff McLaughlin
VP Publisher Roger Shaw
Associate Publisher Thom O'Hearn
Executive Editor Edward Ash-Milby
Assistant Editor Kayla Belser
Production Editor Ivy Long
Art Director Megan Sinead Bingham
Production Designer Jean Hwang
VP Manufacturing Alix Nicholaeff
Production Manager Deena Hashem
Strategic Production Planner Lina s Palma-Temena

Photographer Erin Scott
Food Stylist Lillian Kang
Food Stylist Assistants Paige Arnett and Allee Cakmis

Weldon Owen would also like to thank Karen Levy and Ellen Foreman.

ISBN: 979-8-88674-270-1

Williams Sonoma Custom Edition ISBN: 979-8-88674-506-1

Manufactured in China by Insight Editions
10 9 8 7 6 5 4 3 2 1

ROOTS of PEACE   REPLANTED PAPER

Insight Editions, in association with Roots of Peace, will plant two trees for each tree used in the manufacturing of this book. Roots of Peace is an internationally renowned humanitarian organization dedicated to eradicating land mines worldwide and converting war-torn lands into productive farms and wildlife habitats. Roots of Peace will plant two million fruit and nut trees in Afghanistan and provide farmers there with the skills and support necessary for sustainable land use.